A
FREE MAN
OF COLOR AND
HIS HOTEL

Related Potomac Titles

Father of the Tuskegee Airmen, John C. Robinson,
by Phillip Thomas Tucker

The Most Famous Woman in Baseball: Effa Manley and the Negro Leagues,
by Bob Luke

My Life and Battles, by Jack Johnson,
translated and edited by Christopher Rivers

*One Marshal's Badge: A Memoir of Fugitive Hunting, Witness Protection,
and the U.S. Marshals Service,* by Louie McKinney, with Pat Russo

A

FREE MAN

OF COLOR AND

HIS HOTEL

*Race, Reconstruction, and the Role
of the Federal Government*

CAROL GELDERMAN

Potomac Books
Washington, D.C.

Library of Congress Cataloging-in-Publication Data
Gelderman, Carol W.
    A free man of color and his hotel : race, Reconstruction, and the role of the federal government / Carol Gelderman. — 1st ed.
        p. cm.
    Includes bibliographical references and index.
    ISBN 978-1-59797-833-0 (hardcover : acid-free paper)
    ISBN 978-1-59797-834-7 (electronic edition)
    1. Wormley, James, 1819–1884. 2. Free African Americans—Washington (D.C.)—Biography. 3. African Americans—Washington (D.C.)—Biography. 4. Hotelkeepers—Washington (D.C.)—Biography. 5. Wormley Hotel (Washington, D.C.) 6. Washington (D.C.)—Biography. 7. Reconstruction (U.S. history, 1865–1877)—Washington (D.C.) 8. Washington (D.C.)—Race relations—History—19th century. 9. African Americans—Segregation—History—19th century. 10. African Americans-Government policy—History—19th century. I. Title.
    F198.W83G45 2012
    647.94092—dc23
    [B]
                        2011041712

Printed in the United States of America on acid-free paper that meets the American National Standards Institute Z39-48 Standard.

Potomac Books
22841 Quicksilver Drive
Dulles, Virginia 20166

First Edition

10 9 8 7 6 5 4 3 2 1

CONTENTS

NOTE ON TERMS

Today, U.S. residents who are persons of color are commonly referred to as blacks or African Americans. During the time span of this book, as well as for a century and half before and more than a half a century after, the terms used were Negroes and colored people. I shall, in this book, mainly employ terms in use in the nineteenth century.

PREFACE

*N*ear the end of the American Revolution, the thirteen former colonies joined together in a "firm league of friendship" and drew up the Articles of Confederation, a plan of government for the new United States of America that emphasized the sovereignty of each state. Because the Confederation Congress, made up of delegates from each of the thirteen states, had no power to tax or to settle disputes, even rebellion, it was utterly ineffective in governing the new Republic. The delegates decided that to preserve their young nation, they must revise the articles. Accordingly, fifty-five men from twelve of the original thirteen states (Rhode Island refused to send representatives) spent the hot summer of 1787 in Philadelphia forging a new plan of government. Out of these deliberations came the U.S. Constitution, wholly created by compromise in the ongoing disputes over the proper relationship between national and state power. Arguments over how to protect the interests of both small and large states, for example, nearly wrecked the convention. After delegates agreed on a plan that provided for equal representation in the Senate and representation proportionate to population in the House of Representatives, the big question left was how to count slaves in determining the number of congressmen a state should have.

The Northern states argued that slaves should not be counted. Southerners wanted to count all slaves. The convention compromised. Three-fifths of the slaves would be counted. Because this compromise gave the South a political advantage, slaveholding presidents governed the nation for fifty of its first seventy-two years. In another compromise between North and South, delegates agreed that the foreign slave trade could not be prohibited until 1808.

Constitutional compromise brought relative harmony, but not for long. By adding massive real estate to the country, the 1803 Louisiana Purchase brought the free-state/slave-state issue to a head. Although New York and New England had nearly sixty thousand more free inhabitants than did the entire slaveholding South, the South had thirteen more seats in the House of Representatives and twenty-one more electoral votes. If the Louisiana Territory were opened to slaves, this imbalance would increase. Every new state meant two more Senate votes and a proportional number of House votes. If new land equaled new states, the existing slave states wanted these new territories to become slave states as well. When Missouri applied for statehood in 1817, the slavery debate escalated.

Slavery proved to be impossible to contain within the system. This does not mean legislators did not try. They tried in 1820, they tried in 1833, and again in 1850; they tried yet again in 1854 with the Kansas-Nebraska Act, which allowed settlers of Kansas and Nebraska to vote on whether to allow slavery in the new states. In 1860 and 1861 eleven Southern states carried states' rights to its most extreme by seceding from the Union: "We, the people of the Confederate States, each state acting in its sovereign and independent character . . . do ordain and establish this Constitution for the Confederate States of America." During the Civil War, at Gettysburg, Lincoln spoke a mere 272 words that changed the nation forever. He connected the birth of the United States of America to the Declaration of Independence of 1776, rather than to the Constitution of 1787 with its implicit recognition of slavery, making it clear that America was one nation and not merely a collection of sovereign states. At the end of the Civil War, the Thirteenth Amendment officially abolished and prohibited slavery within the United States. During Reconstruction Congress passed the Civil Rights Acts of 1866 and 1875, declaring Negroes citizens and denying states the power to restrict their rights.

Lincoln's revolutionary address at Gettysburg, in conjunction with Reconstruction's three amendments, gave the country a fundamentally new constitution. The Thirteenth, Fourteenth, and Fifteenth Amendments abolished slavery and gave Negro males civil rights and the vote, and more important, established a *national* citizenship whose rights, enforced by the federal government, were to be enjoyed by all Americans. But the Supreme Court, beginning in 1873, progressively restricted the rights protected under these amendments. By the end of the century, the states had been given carte blanche to circumvent the Reconstruction amendments and the civil rights law. And so matters would rest until the middle of the twentieth century. It seems ironic that the Constitution explains in considerable detail the powers of Congress and the executive branch, while the article on the Supreme Court simply sketches the outline of a federal judiciary in three brief, succinct sections; and yet in three decisions in the 1870s this branch was able to undo the Reconstruction amendments. The brevity of the Constitution's discussion of the court notwithstanding, its power of judicial review was unquestioned. In 1803 *Marbury v. Madison* established the right of the judicial branch of government to declare a law unconstitutional. So a mere five years after passage of the Fourteenth Amendment, the Supreme Court justices set the course of race relations back by retreating from the idea of a strong national government protecting the rights of American citizens, thereby reestablishing the preeminence of states' sovereignty. In so doing the justices effectively annulled Negroes' civil rights.

By 1876 the United States of America, despite successive state/union crises, had reached the centennial of its nationhood, yet it was on the verge of a second civil war a mere eleven years after the first. What precipitated the cataclysm was a presidential election.

The method of choosing a president had been yet another compromise adopted by the draftees of the Constitution in 1787. A principal weakness of the Articles of Confederation was the lack of a single executive. Controversy between those who wanted a strong executive, the presidentialists, and those who saw the need for a strong national legislature, the congressionalists, remained unresolved until the end of the drafting process. A compromise provided for the indirect election of a president by an electoral college. Each state, in a manner directed by its own legislature, must appoint the same number of electors as it had senators and representatives in Congress. Voters, then, voted indirectly for president by voting for his electors. The compromise won support because it decreed that the president would be selected by electors, thereby satisfying both the presidentialists, who had opposed appointment by Congress, and the congressionalists, who had been wary of direct election by the masses.

Great differences separate today's America and the America of the Founding Fathers, yet the debate over the federalist system has remained largely the same. The Constitution was clearly intended to establish a national government, yet nowhere is the word "national" used. It frequently mentions states and the United States but offers nothing precise as to the relationship between the two levels of government. Thus began the enduring debate over the nature of American federalism. From George Washington and Chief Justice John Marshall to Abraham Lincoln and Franklin Roosevelt, there have been those who support a nation-centered federalism—that is, the primacy of the union in this relationship. Others, from Thomas Jefferson and John C. Calhoun to Ronald Reagan and Chief Justice William Rehnquist, fearing centralized government, have been proponents of states' rights.

"Thank God for the limitations inherent in our federal system," wrote Justice Louis Brandeis in the 1920s. "Conflict between federal and state authority means 'vibrations of power,' and this is the genius of our government."[1]

Maybe so, but this conflict between federal and state authority caused a Civil War, the South embodying the ultimate expression of states' rights—secession—and the North guided by a belief in the sanctity of the Union. This book focuses on the aftermath: the dismantling of Reconstruction, which had brought the Thirteenth, Fourteenth, and Fifteenth Amendments, by the Supreme Court's undoing of the federal protections guaranteed by these amendments; the resultant contested election of 1876; and the loss of civil rights protection for another eighty years.

By intertwining the story of a successful Negro businessman who grabbed the opportunity that the short-lived primacy of federal protection offered with the consequences of three decisions of the Supreme Court and a watershed election, I try to show why it matters that the federal government protects citizens' rights, not only for the individual but pragmatically for the country. One can only wonder how many other potential Negro successes were lost during the long segregation era that followed the election. Historians know how those losses affected the country; "the federal courts," to take one example from Eric Foner's remarkable synthesis of the history of Reconstruction, "used the greatly expanded jurisdiction born of Reconstruction primarily to protect corporations from local regulation" rather than people's rights.[2] In other words, the Republican Party, which called itself the Union Party in 1864, became the party of property rights.

Chapter 1 introduces James Wormley, who, because federal legislation now protected Negroes' civil rights, had managed to own and operate Washington, D.C.'s most luxurious hotel at a time when most financial and governmental business was conducted in hotels.

Chapter 2 lays out the main issue of the 1876 election, namely reform owing to two scandal-ridden Grant administrations. Democrats, because of railroad lawyer Samuel Tilden of New York, had the first chance of winning the presidency since secession. Tilden became the man of the hour for overthrowing the notorious William "Boss" Tweed, whose ring had stolen millions from the New York City treasury, and as a result was elected governor of New York in 1874. Once again he overthrew another corrupt ring, this one statewide, and became a reform hero admired all over the country.

Chapter 3 introduces Washington, D.C.'s "Boss," Alexander Shepherd, a man who almost single-handedly turned the backwater District of Columbia into a city worthy of being the capital of the industrial giant that America would become, and in so doing created work for the city's huge Negro population. This chapter follows Wormley's continued success despite the action of the Supreme Court in reasserting states' rights.

Chapter 4 details an election that brought the country close to another war owing to the Supreme Court decisions that emasculated federal protection of people's rights. If Negro voting rights had been federally protected, then Democrat Tilden would never have carried the South.

Chapter 5 describes the Centennial Exposition in Philadelphia to which James Wormley was invited, a six-month event celebrating the almost miraculous but uncertain survival of the United States given its still unresolved contested presidential election.

Chapter 6 provides the resolution of the election, but not until March 2, 1877, two days before President Grant's term expired.

Chapter 7 shows the effects of the end of Reconstruction up to and including the Supreme Court's *Plessy v. Ferguson* decision that made segregation legal. After 1877 the idea of a strong national government protecting the rights of American citizens, an idea born in the early days of the nation and reborn during and after the Civil War, lay impotent.

James Wormley died in 1884. James T. Wormley took over the management of the hotel after his father's death, but the total disenfranchisement of Negroes prompted him to sell in 1893. The new owner operated under the Wormley name until 1897.

The epilogue describes the numerous parallels between the era of Wormley's Hotel and our own in terms of judicial conservatism, financial corruption, and the widening gulf between the haves and have-nots.

WHAT MIGHT HAVE BEEN

Ours is a monstrous system. . . . Like the patriarchs of old our men live all in one house with their wives and their concubines, and the mulattos one sees in every family exactly resemble the white children and every lady tells you who is the father of all the mulatto children in everybody's household, but those in her own; she seems to think they drop from the clouds.

  —Mary Boykin Chesnut, diary
   March 18, 1861

*E*arly in 1927 a woman who identified herself as a Wormeley of the Virginia Wormeleys made arrangements to interview various Washington Wormleys in order to compile a family genealogy. The Wormeleys, because they had acquired vast land grants before 1700, had been one of the wealthiest and most powerful of the Virginia colonial families. This Wormeley descendant and a granddaughter traveled from Urbanna, a town ten miles up the Rappahannock River from Chesapeake Bay, and the site of what had once been the family's plantation, Rosegill, to the nation's capital. The two ladies interviewed five of the grandchildren of the well-known nineteenth-century hotel proprietor, James Wormley. Wormley's Hotel was the most luxurious in the city in an era during which hotels played a significant role in politics and government. "Most European royalty stay

1

at Wormley's Hotel. Why haven't you, Princess," asks a character in Gore Vidal's novel *1876*,[1] just as other characters comment that "it's the only *nice* place, really."[2]

The two visitors, because of James Wormley's renown, had been curious about the Washington line of the family and wished to know more about them. Their meeting led to a second, which, like the first, proceeded in a friendly manner. Unexpectedly, however, the older Virginian said that if she got to the point of publishing her genealogy, she was sure the Washington Wormleys would understand if there was no mention of their branch of the family. The nephew of one of the persons present wrote about what happened next:

> At that point, Jessie A. Wormley, a small woman, stood up proudly to her full five feet and said that the facts of history were unalterable and could not be omitted, discarded, or changed by whim simply because you may not like them. She was a perfect lady and a college professor, whose English was beautiful, and I could not have been more proud of her as at this moment. She quickly but firmly let the visitors know that she would accept facts but not condescensions and chicanery and finally said, "I think we [have] reached the point that this interview is terminated."[3]

The Wormeley surname first shows up in Britain in the early Middle Ages. It means "one who comes from Wormley, that is, a wood infested with reptiles."[4] A small farming village located on the old North Road in Hertfordshire, Wormley flourished even before the four-hundred-year Roman dominion in the British Isles. Yet the first Wormleys on record hailed from County Cheshire north and west of Hertfordshire. The first record of a Wormley dates from the reign of Edward the Confessor (1042–1066), the last Anglo-Saxon king of England. When William the Conqueror ordered a survey of the country in 1086, the name Wormley appeared frequently in the first Domesday Book. Sir Nicholas de Wormele and Petri de Wormeleye appeared in various "inquisitions of the twelfth and thirteenth centuries,"[5] and in 1312 Sir John de Wormele, Knight, was deeded lands in Hatfield, Fishlake, and the Park of Eshefield in Yorkshire. These grants were confirmed and added to by King Edward III in 1341. After this point the name is recorded in an unbroken line from father to son for sixteen generations. From the time of Queen Elizabeth I the spelling of the name alternated between Wormley and Wormeley.

The first Wormeleys in America were brothers Christopher and Ralphe, the fifteenth generation descended from Sir John de Wormele of Hatfield. The brothers reached Virginia in the mid-1630s. Both had received large land grants from the crown and both became prominent in the governance of the colony, but it was Ralphe who became the progenitor of sons who perpetuated the family surname on this side of the Atlantic. Already the owner of thousands of acres in the colony, Ralphe received in 1649 an additional crown grant of thirteen thousand acres of the best land in what is now Middlesex County.

Middlesex, a Tidewater county in the Rappahannock River Valley area, is one of twelve counties in Virginia named after English shires. Middlesex was perhaps the most influential colony in the King's Council and the House of Burgesses, and furnished members of both bodies and, during a fifty-three-year tenure, three receiver-generals, the custodians of all of the colony's revenue. No other county in the colony controlled the finances of Virginia for so long. Middlesex also provided two presidents of the King's Council, one being Ralphe Wormeley. For many years he also served as secretary of state for the Virginia colony.

Ralphe Wormeley built the well-known colonial manor Rosegill in Middlesex in 1650. Situated on a gentle bluff that overlooks the broad reaches of the Rappahannock River ten miles from Chesapeake Bay, Rosegill became one of the best-known houses in the colony. It was rare that a distinguished Englishman came to Virginia and returned home without visiting Rosegill. In colonial times two long lines of giant roses followed a walk to the river's edge. The main house had been built between two smaller buildings designed to look like large English cottages. One became a school, the other the kitchen. Each had a gabled roof, dormer windows, and chimneys at both ends. The formal entrance faced the river, although visitors entered the grounds through double gates on the land side of the house and walked down a long line of cherry trees that stopped just short of the main house.

Rosegill was home to five generations of Wormeleys, each important in the hierarchy of the colony and connected with every great house in Virginia. Over the next half century the Wormeleys, along with such families as the Fitzhughs, Byrds, Carters, Lees, Randolphs, Harrisons, Digges, and Nelsons, laid the foundations of their fortunes in vast land grants.[6] These "best" families tended to intermarry so that by the beginning of the eighteenth century not more than a hundred families controlled the wealth and government of the colony. Virginia had become an aristocracy that imitated England. "It was as if the landed families of Virginia," historian Daniel Boorstin wrote in *The Americans: The Colonial Experience*, "had brought with them the text of a drama long played on the English stage which now would be played on the American."[7]

Ralphe Wormeley even dressed like an Englishman, wearing a cocked hat, knee breeches, and low quarter shoes with silver buckles. To complete the English picture, he frequently appeared in a coach and four with a liveried driver and coachman, a mode of travel bound to attract comment in sparsely populated Middlesex. Ralphe Wormeley died in 1651, leaving his widow with two infant sons. The widow then married Sir Henry Chicheley, who, even after he became governor of the colony, lived at Rosegill, going back and forth to Jamestown, for, as a historian of Middlesex County asked, "Who is it would not prefer the crystal waters and unsurpassed oysters of the Rappahannock to those of the murky waters of the noble James?"[8] When the second American Ralph Wormeley turned fourteen in 1665, his mother took him to England and placed him in Oriel College, Oxford, thereby making him the first Virginia resident to matriculate at an English university. He returned to Virginia with an extraordinary collection of four thousand books. After acquiring thousands of additional acres, Ralph II enlarged and embellished the houses on the estate. By the time he had finished, the mansion boasted a chapel, picture gallery, enormous library, thirty guest chambers plus fourteen beds in the attic for visiting bachelors, a handsome drawing room with eight-panel doors, paneled walls, a Sienna marble mantel, and a twelve-foot-wide entrance hall. In 1686 a French Huguenot immigrant, M. Durand de Dauphine, described Rosegill as "at least twenty houses along a plateau above the river."[9] The main house was eighty-seven feet long and forty feet wide with a Dutch roof, a washhouse, and two brick wings thirty-three by twenty-two feet and one story high each, connected to the main house by an eighty-six-by-nine-foot covered walk.

In addition to his wealth, Ralph II was powerful, serving as a member of the House of Burgesses, a member of the King's Council, a secretary of state, president of the council, and acting governor of the colony. Moreover, as one of the founders of William and Mary College, he remained a trustee for life. Yet despite his prominent role in the governance of the colony, he refused to sell the fifty acres Middlesex County had designated to become the future town of Urbanna and the home of an official tobacco inspection center. From Virginia's first assembly in 1619, acts were passed providing for inspection of tobacco at authorized places so that its quality might be improved and frauds in payments prevented. All tobacco had to be brought to warehouses, inspected, and stamped. Such was the commercial value of these inspection centers that county officials forced Ralph II to release fifty acres; thus was the town of Urbanna founded in 1680.

Following family tradition, Ralph Wormeley III offered his services to the county, working as Middlesex sheriff during 1704 and 1705, but he died shortly after. His brother John inherited the estate. Like his progenitors, John attended English schools, and he, too, died young. He did, however, leave an heir, Ralph IV, who increased the family's wealth. Called the King of Virginia, he sent his own ship to England each year, full of tobacco grown on his land, which he increased by buying eight thousand acres on the right bank of Shenandoah, west of Harper's Ferry in Frederick County. Uneasy about his purchase, he consulted his friend George Washington. "Keep the land," Washington said. "I have surveyed it, and I know it to be as fine a tract as any in Virginia. But if you really want to get rid of it, I will take it off your hands."[10] Thus reassured, Ralph IV held on to the property and built a shooting box on it for hunting. His son, Ralph V, was confined to the Frederick land for two years for being a "malignant Tory."

Maybe because Ralph V had stayed on in England after graduation from Eton and Cambridge, "living among the wits of Johnson's time,"[11] he was reluctant to return to Virginia, doing so only at his father's behest shortly before the Revolution. Not long after his return in April 1776, he was arrested and examined at Williamsburg by a Committee of Safety. A letter Ralph V had written to neighbor and close friend John Grymes had been intercepted, and in the committee's opinion it afforded "full proof of Wormeley's enmity to the Whigs and a readiness to join their enemies whenever called upon."[12] What led to this turn of events was a proclamation issued by Lord Dunmore, Royal Governor of Virginia, in November 1775 that freed any slave who joined His Majesty's troops. Dunmore's edict impelled the Continental Congress to action. It urged Virginians to resist Dunmore to the hilt. During skirmishes between the British and Virginia militia, Dunmore left the mainland for a ship anchored in Chesapeake Bay and asked Wormeley to attend him on board. Wormeley refused and then wrote Grymes the letter that led to his arrest. In a petition to the Virginia Convention expressing deep regret that "he had drawn the odium of the country on him,"[13] he stated his strong views that the British parliament had no right to tax America. Still, he differed with his fellow Virginians on their method of dealing with the mother country. Despite his plea, the Virginia Convention decided that Ralph Wormeley V showed an unfriendly disposition that was dangerous to their rights and that he should be confined to the county of Frederick and give a 20,000-pound bond not to depart from those limits. His father, Ralph IV, who also sided with the English but who had the sense to keep quiet about his feelings, provided the bond. Ralph V remained in confinement on his father's hunting property until 1778, when he returned to Rosegill. Ironically, three years later, this "malignant Tory" suffered heavy losses, including thirty-six slaves, when Frederick Rhinelander, a Tory privateer from New York, attacked the estate. Eventually Ralph V regained the confidence of the people of his county and was several times elected a member of the House of Delegates and a member of the Convention of 1788. The 1790 census shows that 320 slaves then resided at Rosegill plantation.[14] Yet, a short sixteen years later, Ralph V's estate lists only twenty-four slaves.[15]

The "rehabilitated" Ralph was the last Wormeley to occupy Rosegill. After he died in 1806, he left his widow Eleanor Tayloe, "a very silly woman," according to a distant cousin,[16] and their seven children well off. His three sons, however, lost everything because, as the same cousin said, they were "given to dissipation. They squandered the estate which lavish hospitalities had encumbered." All of the land and buildings passed out of the family and fell into decay. Much later, Rosegill became a tobacco storehouse.

The Wormeley name, too, might have disappeared had Ralph V not also sired at least two children, Lynch and William, by an unidentified colored woman. William had at least one child, but Lynch had many children, who had many children on through generations, all successful to this day. It is as if the Wormeley genes got a new current that took the family to fresh heights. The earliest of these Wormleys—the first "e" in the surname disappeared in the colored branch of the family—lacked any of the advantages of the white Wormeleys, yet by emigrating to Washington City and by working hard, both Lynch and William prospered.

No birth certificate for Lynch has ever been found, but the 1850 U.S. Census lists Lynch Wormley as being seventy years old, which means he was probably born in 1780. Very little information has survived about the lives of colored families during the federal city's early years. City directories, which appeared first in 1822, listed residents' race, occupations, and addresses, an occasional item in the city's newspaper, the *National Intelligencer*, and fleeting allusions in travelers' descriptions of the capital supply a skimpy picture of their lives. The letters and diaries of white Washingtonians rarely mentioned colored people; visitors, if they noticed anything at all about the Negro, commented on the slave pens and auction blocks that spilled over into the backyard of the White House. In fact, before the Civil War, the District of Columbia had the most active slave depots in the nation.[17]

What is known about life among Negroes before the Civil War must be drawn from word-of-mouth reminiscences.

When the District of Columbia was created in 1790, more than half of the country's Negroes lived in the states from which it was carved: Maryland and Virginia. Not surprisingly, the new federal district had an unusually large number of colored residents, a quarter of the population by the time Lynch and William arrived in 1814. When they got to the capital, the city lay in ruins. In late August the British had entered Washington, burned the Capitol and the White House, demolished Potomac Bridge, the War and Treasury Buildings, and the arsenal at Greenleaf's Point. At the same time a tornado struck the city, ripping the rooftops off houses and creating a general mass of debris. The double disaster was in one sense fortunate in that it created abundant jobs for the Negro population in the building trades and in service occupations. Because thirty-four-year-old Lynch Wormley had come to the city with his wife, Mary (sometimes called Cleo), and their seven children, he needed work desperately. Lynch managed to find a modest two-room house on E Street, only a few short blocks from John Tayloe III's magnificent Octagon House built by William Thornton, the first architect of the U.S. Capitol, and the home where President James Madison and his wife, Dolley, lived while the White House was being rebuilt—which turned out to be the remainder of Madison's second administration. In February of 1815 Madison signed the Treaty of Ghent, ending the War of 1812, in the Octagon House with owner John Tayloe and his family present. Although Tayloe was the brother-in-law of Lynch Wormley's father, Ralph, it is unlikely John Tayloe and Lynch Wormley ever crossed paths.

Not until 1818 is there an official record of Lynch's employment, namely that he had tried to purchase a carriage and harness from a local livery owner but never concluded the transaction.[18] Although Lynch had agreed to pay $175 in monthly installments of ten dollars, the seller took him to court after nine payments to take back his carriage. Why is not clear. In March 1820 Lynch's name shows up again, this time for having secured "free papers" for $400 from J. P. Cocke. This official fact presents something of a dilemma: if Lynch considered himself free and lived as if free, why would he pay to obtain papers attesting to his free status?

According to Wormley family tradition, Lynch was born free, and facts support this belief. In Virginia law a manumitted slave had to leave the state within twelve months or be re-enslaved.[19] Yet Lynch had lived free in Virginia for three and a half decades, and another half decade in Washington before procuring "free" papers.

Living in D.C. for a free Negro could be dangerous. After the 1808 constitutional prohibition on importation of Africans into the United States took effect, Washington became one of the principal slave markets in the nation. Franklin and Armfield, one of the most efficient and profitable of the slave marketing firms, conducted most of its business in the city. Capitalizing on the steady reduction of tobacco cultivation in Maryland and Virginia, which provided a growing surplus of slaves, the firm regularly sent ships of these slaves to the New Orleans market to provide labor for the new cotton and sugar plantations in the Deep South. Slave pens were established behind Decatur House on Lafayette Square and next to the Capitol. When the pens were full, the city jails became holding centers for slaves awaiting transfer south. So lucrative was this business that it was common for even free Negroes to be seized and transported to an auction block. Besides Lynch's brother, William, and his family, Lynch and Mary had ten children by 1820. So large a family as the Wormleys represented a sizeable fortune to the slave traders. Yet no move had ever been made to take any of the Wormleys. It appeared they were safe from seizure, despite Lynch's not having a certificate of freedom that provided protection from kidnapping.

Two twentieth-century Wormleys conducted an exhaustive search to discover the connection between J. P. Cocke and Lynch Wormley.[20] They found numerous references to the Cocke family in state, county, and historical society libraries. They located family papers, Bibles, reminiscences, biographies, several family stories of the time, slave lists, white and colored indentured servant lists, personal property lists, and other similar-type ledgers. J. P. Cocke and members of his family were alike in their meticulous record-keeping. In all of this memorabilia and documentary evidence, not a single mention of Lynch or Mary or of the Wormley family shows up.

Possibly, then, the 1820 "free papers" were connected in some way to the periodic tightening of the Black Codes that regulated the lives of free persons of color. Because the Black Codes were far more restrictive in the rest of the South, Washington officials feared that Negroes would swarm into the capital, so periodically they tightened the codes. The city's first Black Code was enacted in 1808. Under this law, no Negro could be on the street after ten p.m. Every few years penalties for breaking the curfew were increased, and by 1812 free people of color had to register and carry a certificate of freedom. No matter how harsh the codes became—for example, one-year-free Negroes were required to post a $500 bond guaranteed by two white men—the Wormleys seemed unaffected.

The free papers, therefore, served only one purpose—to enable Lynch Wormley to obtain a license to own a hackney carriage.[21] He had tried to buy a carriage and harness in 1818 and failed; by 1821 he had the "right" papers, apparently, and succeeded. He could not acquire proof of freedom from his deceased father, although he could show two letters written by Ralph Wormeley, one to the governor of Maryland reporting the sailing of a schooner outfitted by a privateer in Charleston and asking the governor to be vigilant, and the other discussing the sale of the plantation.[22] He thus procured free papers from J. P. Cocke in March of 1820 for $400. Whether this money was actually paid is not known. Sometimes sympathetic whites issued such papers without charge.

From 1821 on, and maybe before, Lynch Wormley supported his large family by driving a hackney carriage. Lynch had chosen the best possible profession for a Negro. First, it exempted him from the ten p.m. curfew. Second, it enabled him to operate his own business, an opportunity not allowed Negroes in any other undertaking. Third, it gave Lynch the opportunity to meet and get to know members of the federal and local government, bankers, and other businessmen of the community. Finally, Lynch carried information from one influential person to another, a social and economic opportunity not afforded other Negroes, and Lynch made the most of these favorable circumstances.

According to the testimony of visitors to Washington, hackmen made a great deal of money. One traveler reported that during his stay in the capital, he spent thirty dollars a week on cab fares, while an English visitor claimed that during one night alone he spent twenty-five dollars for transportation. Another tourist commented that Washington "was the very paradise of hackney coachmen. . . . If these men do not get rich it must be owing to some culpable extravagance, for their vehicles are in continuous demand from the hour of dinner until five in the morning, and long distances and heavy charges are all in their favor."[23]

If having a wife and ten children was "culpable extravagance," then Lynch Wormley had to plead guilty, yet by the mid-1820s he was operating a good-sized livery stable at Fifteenth Street and Pennsylvania Avenue, NW, near the Willard Hotel. In due time he bought several pieces of property on I Street between Fifteenth and Sixteenth Streets, NW. His son John also owned property on I Street, property that he had earned by working for Susan Decatur, the widow of the naval war hero Stephen Decatur. When Decatur died in a duel in 1820, he left his widow little money, but a great deal of land, including an elegant townhouse designed by Benjamin Latrobe across from the White House on the northwest corner of Lafayette Square. In 1830 Mrs. Decatur transferred an I Street lot she owned to Mary Wormley as payment for services John Wormley had provided. Lynch and Mary deeded this lot to John. The deed, dated March 26, 1831, shows that Lynch was probably illiterate, as he marked his signature with an X.

By mid-century Lynch Wormley owned so much property on I Street that the alley behind it became known as Wormley Alley. The property remained in the family for decades as each member who died either left the land to children or to another family member. Matilda Conners Wormley, the widow of Lynch's brother, William, for example, "bequeathed her lot of ground with frame house" to a daughter-in-law, who in turn left the house to her daughter.[24]

Tax records show that by 1845 Lynch owned property in several places in the city, including the Liberia Hotel, located on E Street between Fourteenth and Fifteenth Streets, NW. The Union League Directory called the Liberia "quite pretentious" for the times because the capital required for building and maintaining the establishment ranged somewhere between fifteen and twenty-five thousand dollars. That Lynch had done well by hackney driving is clear; that three of his sons took up hacking is not surprising; what is odd is the name of his hotel. In the early 1800s the American Colonization Society was formed in the United States to take freed Negroes back to Africa. The society bought land in an area named Liberia, which lies just north of the equator where the west coast of Africa bulges out into the Atlantic Ocean. The society made its first settlement in 1822 in the city called Monrovia after then-president James Monroe. Few free people of color, if any, wanted to be transplanted to an alien land, and Lynch Wormley, born on American soil, was no exception. Why, then, he called his "pretentious" hotel the Liberia is puzzling. That he had invested in the hotel business at age sixty-five may have inspired his ninth child, James, whose own eponymous hotel would place the Wormley name in the annals of Reconstruction history.

James Wormley, the ninth of Mary and Lynch Wormley's ten children, was born on January 16, 1819, in a small brick building owned by his parents on E Street near Fourteenth Street, NW. At the time of his birth the house had two good-sized rooms plus an attic and a cellar for storage. While James was still a toddler, his oldest brother, William, nineteen years his elder, worked as a hacker for their father, Lynch. In 1823, when James was four, William obtained a license to own two hackney carriages to set up his own livery and hack driving business. At the same time William got to know Mary Hall, a white woman who was a member of the Society of Friends and who ran a school for free children of color in a house on Fifteenth Street. Since her space only accommodated forty pupils, Mrs. Hall was forced to be very selective. William made sure that James was one of the forty. In 1824, at five years of age, James started school.

Impressed by Mrs. Hall's influence, William sent his sister Mary, at great expense, to Philadelphia to the Colored Female Seminary, which was then in the charge of Miss Sara Douglass, an accomplished Quaker woman of color. When Mary graduated, William built a schoolhouse for her near the corner of Vermont Avenue and I Street. No sooner had Mary got the school going in 1830, when James was eleven, than she got sick. An English gentleman by the name of Calvert took over her classes. James had him for a teacher. In 1834, shortly before Mary died in 1835, William Thomas Lee took over the school.[25]

By this time William's livery stable, one of the largest and best in the city, had made him wealthy and well-known. When abolitionists William Lloyd Garrison and Isaac Knapp launched their newspaper, the *Liberator*, in 1831, William Wormley became its agent for the District. Eight months later Nat Turner's Rebellion occurred in Southampton County, Virginia, which Southern whites attributed to the influence of Garrison's paper. Beginning on August 21, 1831, and continuing for three days, Turner and six of his friends started a rampage of premeditated, brutal, and unmerciful killing of whites, fifty-seven in all, freeing slaves as they went. The band of seven grew to some seventy or eighty slaves. Not until November 11 was Turner captured and executed by hanging. Even Georgetown citizens started seeing abolitionists as dangerous agitators. For the first time ever, Georgetown enacted a black code, listing among punishable Negro offenses the possession of literature "calculated to excite insurrection or insubordination among the slaves or colored people . . . and particularly a newspaper called *The Liberator*."[26] Slave states denounced Garrison and the paper he edited, outlawing abolitionist societies and literature. In Washington, Congress debated various abolitionist petitions, which Garrison published in the *Liberator*. "Senator John C. Calhoun of South Carolina leveled murderous charges against us," Garrison wrote, "crying that the abolitionist attack was an all-out war against the south and that the petitions should not even be received" by Congress.[27] At that point former president and current representative John Quincy Adams of Massachusetts rose in eloquent defense of the right of American citizens to petition their government. "But in an act of high handed despotism," Garrison wrote, "the House adopted the 'gag rule,' or 'Pinckney gag,' proposed by Representative Henry L. Pinckney of South Carolina, which automatically tabled abolitionist petitions, and the Senate also voted to table them." Garrison ended his argument by declaring that the adoption of the gag rule made him doubt that "slavery could ever be abolished by political action, the Federal Government being so completely dominated and polluted by Slave Power."

Tensions in Washington ran high, reaching the breaking point in 1835 when word spread that a young slave, Arthur Bowen, had become inflamed by abolitionist propaganda and tried to kill the widow of William Thornton, the same Thornton who had designed the Capitol and the Octagon House. On the night of April 11 a mob of young white manual laborers wrecked a restaurant at Sixth and Pennsylvania Avenue owned by Beverly Snow, a free colored man. Snow escaped unharmed to Canada, and the marauding, which continued for the next two days, came to be called the Snow Riot. Next, the mob went after William Wormley, the Washington agent of the *Liberator*. With the warning and help of friends, Wormley managed to take refuge in Pennsylvania, but the gang destroyed his sister's school and plundered and set fire to the homes of other prominent free persons of color, their churches, and their schools. Like William Wormley, the well-known Negro minister and educator John F. Cook escaped by horseback to Pennsylvania. The reign of terror, for so it proved to be in a community where the entire police force consisted of three men, did not come to an end until the mayor directed the city council to restore peace and quiet, and ordered Negroes off the streets at night. President Andrew Jackson gave notice that the fugitives who returned to the city would be protected. William Wormley returned, but to persecution so persistent that his health and business sank under its effects. Mary Wormley's schoolhouse was restored, but William died a poor man. It was left to his younger brother James to restore the family position.

At the time of the Snow Riot, James Wormley was seventeen, out of school, and working full time for his father, driving a hackney carriage. By early 1841 he had saved enough money to marry seventeen-year-old Anna Elizabeth Thompson of Virginia. In the next eight years James and Anna became parents to William Henry Ashburton Wormley, born April 10, 1842; James Thompson Wormley, born February 14, 1844; Garrett Smith Wormley (named for the wealthy New York abolitionist Gerrit Smith), born on April 12, 1846, the same year that Alexandria retrocessed to Virginia; and Anna Matilda Wormley, born in 1850.

In addition to caring for four infants, Anna Wormley operated a confectionary store, and James worked a variety of jobs in order to gain experience and make contacts. He served as a boat steward on a U.S. vessel and on a Mississippi River boat, and he tried prospecting for gold in California during the gold rush years. By the early 1850s he believed he was ready for his real calling: he opened and operated a catering business next door to his wife's confectionary on I Street. Washington in the 1850s offered caterers ample opportunity to make good money. Most senators and representatives lived in Washington only during periods when Congress was in session. They lived in the city's many boarding houses and hotels, taking most of their meals in their rooms. Moreover, running the federal government's various departments required a bevy of clerks who also lived in boarding houses. Caterers supplied these boarders with meals at a fixed price per month. For twenty dollars a caterer delivered breakfast every morning and dinner every evening, in a square tin box, for thirty days. So successful was Wormley as a caterer that he was able to purchase his own boarding houses on I Street. Before long he owned and operated four such enterprises in the fifteen hundred block of I Street, NW. An ad, which ran regularly in Washington's papers, cited, "Wormley's Celebrated Dining Rooms at Nos. 310, 314, 318, and 320 I Street, between Fifteenth and Sixteenth Streets."[28] Uncompromising in his delivery of good service and food, Wormley attracted guests from all over.

"I put up at one of the lodging houses of Mr. Wormley, a colored man, in I Street," the novelist Anthony Trollope wrote at the end of his month-long stay in Washington City, "to whose attention I can recommend to any Englishman who may chance to want quarters in Washington. My landlord told me he was sorry I was going. Would I not remain? Would I come back to him? Had I been comfortable? Only for so and so or so and so, he would have done better for me. No white American citizen, occupying the position of landlord, would have condescended to such comfortable words. I knew the man did not in truth want me to stay, as a lady and gentleman were waiting to go in the moment I went out, but I did not the less value the assurance."[29]

Though life for the Wormleys was prosperous and predictable, tension in the city grew over the issue of slavery so that by the end of the decade it overshadowed everything else. Just how explosive the situation was became apparent when white abolitionist John Brown, along with twenty-one followers, attacked and captured the federal arsenal at Harpers Ferry, a short sixty-five miles from Washington, on October 16, 1859. Brown called for a slave uprising. After a two-day siege federal soldiers took prisoner those who had not been killed. White Washingtonians panicked. A senator suggested that the city would do better as the capital of an alliance of Southern states rather than of all the states.

Southern sympathy was strong in Washington. A militant political organization of Southerners, the Jackson Democratic Association, had eight hundred members who drilled at night and threatened to seize the capital. President Buchanan sought to organize the Washington militia, but Congress refused to act. The Wormleys clearly had a lot to think about besides business. The commanding general of the U.S. Army, Winfield Scott, lived in rooms he rented from Wormley, and he often talked of his frustration at having only 150 troops in Washington, whose loyalty he doubted.[30] Although a Virginian by birth, Scott believed strongly in the Union. Appearances, however, belied this loyalty. A Southern clique ruled the army: Southern West Pointers headed five of the six army departments, and had Robert E. Lee accepted Scott's offer of the Department of the East, all six would have been commanded by Southerners. As a result, ambitious Northerners who had shown promise at the military academy, men like Henry Halleck, George McClellan, Joseph Hooker, Ambrose Burnside, William Sherman, and William Rosecrans, resigned their commissions and returned to civilian life.[31]

Although Scott had much admired James Wormley and loved his food, he moved during the winter of 1860 to Crutchet at Sixth and D Streets because his new quarters were situated on the ground floor. Scott was seventy-four and walked slowly with pain, so his new location made life easier than it had been in the upper-floor apartment he had occupied at Wormley's. Moreover, Crutchet, a French caterer, was every bit as adept at cooking the general's favorite delicacy, terrapin (freshwater snapping turtle), as was Wormley.

Within days of Lincoln's election in 1860, the South Carolina legislature voted to secede from the Union. Before Lincoln arrived in Washington, five more states seceded: Alabama, Florida, Georgia, Louisiana, and Mississippi. By the time the war began, the first six states of the Confederacy were joined by five more: Texas, Virginia, Arkansas, North Carolina, and Tennessee. Three months passed before the local militia was reorganized and a thousand Washingtonians were armed and in uniform. After Lincoln's inauguration, the citizen soldiery returned to their civilian pursuits. Not until April 15, 1861, did Lincoln issue his first call for Northern troops. Unarmed and ununiformed, men from Pennsylvania, New York, and Massachusetts started arriving in Washington. The city's parks and squares became camping grounds. Forts sprang into existence, and an endless roll of army wagons, ambulances, and marching troops gave Washington the look and feel of the base headquarters of the Union Army.

On November 1, 1861, a thirty-five year old George McClellan replaced the aging Winfield Scott as general of the Union Army. Although brilliant and a good organizer, McClellan turned out to be more of an asset to the South than to the North. Vain, egotistical, paranoid, procrastinating, and snobbish, he seemed more interested in overseeing parades and dawdling around Washington than in fighting. General McClellan took his meals luxuriously at Wormley's, hosting dinners for twenty or more with a wide variety of wines, several times a week.

"This army has got to fight or run away," a disgusted Secretary of War Edwin Stanton declared. "While men are striving nobly in the west, the champagne and oyster suppers on the Potomac must be stopped."[32] Lincoln agreed and demoted McClellan from general-in-chief to commander of the Army of the Potomac. Still McClellan tarried, claiming a need for more training, more troops, more guns, and more preparation. Eight months after demotion McClellan finally yielded to calls by Lincoln to take Richmond, the capital of the Confederacy. On the advance toward Yorktown, Virginia, on the peninsula between the James and York Rivers and only five miles from Richmond, McClellan stopped to request yet more troops. They were sent. Still no military action, but excursion parties from Washington, catered by Wormley, visited White House Landing on the Pamunkey. On one excursion Secretary of State William Seward, Navy Secretary Gideon Welles, Attorney General Edward Bates, and Navy Commander John Dahlgren, accompanied by their wives, made the trip on the steamboat *City of Baltimore*. McClellan drove them around in ambulances. A hospital nurse, one of the Virginia Wormeleys who worked at the headquarters of the United States Sanitary Commission during the peninsular campaign, wrote about these visits of ladies "in silks and perfumes and lilac kid gloves."[33] In Washington people talked of little else; embarrassed by the gossip, McClellan forbade further excursions.

In late June 1862 Robert E. Lee attacked. McClellan responded by retreating, thereby ending the Union threat to Richmond and the possibility of an early end to the war. Demoted once again, he finally confronted Lee at Antietam in Maryland, the bloodiest day of the war. Although the Union lost 12,000 troops to the Confederacy's 11,000, the battle was a Union victory. Sadly, the ever-cautious McClellan failed to pursue Lee, allowing him and his troops to escape across the Potomac and back into Virginia, thereby losing the chance to deal a decisive and finishing blow to the Army of Virginia. Lincoln dismissed McClellan from further command.

While McClellan had been procrastinating on the peninsula, Lincoln emancipated the 3,100 slaves of Washington, D.C., compensating their owners $993,406.

Fugitive slaves from Maryland and Virginia, called contrabands of war,[34] poured into the District. The War Department hired them at forty cents a day to work in the camps and depots around the city. But their numbers grew and grew, so that by the spring of 1863, and despite a devastating smallpox epidemic among their numbers, there were ten thousand contrabands in the city. Their shanties sprang up in the malarial swamps along the canal known as "Murder Bay." The quarter-master of Washington resettled many of them on the captured estate of Robert E. Lee in Alexandria, while the eleven thousand–plus free Negroes in Washington or-ganized relief associations. The Contraband Relief Association set up by Elizabeth Keckley, seamstress to Mary Todd Lincoln, was one of the most effective. Because Keckley traveled all over the Eastern Seaboard with Mrs. Lincoln, she was able to raise a great deal of money, all of which she funneled through James Wormley, who disbursed it. He carried on this humane work while tending to his boarding house clientele at a time when Washington boarding houses were bulging from the hun-dreds of new clerks needed for war-related work (the number of clerks necessary to run a growing federal government grew from less than 300 in 1802 to 2,199 in 1861), to his catering service that operated at full speed (with so many new board-ers needing daily breakfast and dinner), and to his restaurant, which had become one of the most popular meeting places in the city. As if he were not busy enough, at the recommendation of prominent white businessmen George Riggs, William Corcoran, and Louis Clephane, he accepted an appointment as club steward for the newly founded Metropolitan Club. As oddly timed as the founding of a social club appeared, the event was hardly out of the ordinary. As the war grew bloodier, the social pace of official Washington grew more frenetic. "Washington seems crazy," opined one newcomer in early 1863. "Four or five parties in one evening seems the fashion." The correspondent for the *London Times* found the socializing "revolting" at this time of "grievous national calamity."[35]

President Lincoln, however, had remained aloof, all the time weighing the en-listment of Negroes into the Union army, something abolitionists and colored leaders had been urging him to do since the beginning of the war. By spring 1863 the president urged a massive recruitment of Negro troops. "The colored popu-lation is the great *available* and yet *unavailed* of force for restoring the Union," he said, mindful of the great losses of Union men in battle and of the lack of new vol-unteers to take their places.[36] Before the year was out, 166 black regiments, pri-marily infantry, had been formed, even though the colored troops were paid ten dollars a month with no clothing allowance, while whites got thirteen dollars and three dollars and sixty cents a month in clothing allowance. Organized into segregated regiments, they often found themselves subjected to abuse from white officers.

James Wormley's second son, James T., enlisted as a private on March 17, 1864, and mustered into I Company of the Massachusetts Fifth Cavalry, the only regiment of colored cavalry troops in Massachusetts.[37] The regiment included a dozen companies of 1,325 colored men and 61 white officers. Although trained as cavalry, the regiment's first assignment to the third division, eighteenth corps at West Point, Virginia, required infantry service. After several weeks of drill, guard, and picket duty, the regiment faced its first serious engagement on June 15, 1864, at Baylor's Farm on Petersburg Road. Three men died and nineteen suffered serious wounds, one of whom was Maj. Charles Francis Adams Jr., grandson of John Quincy Adams and great-grandson of John Adams. In July Adams was promoted to lieutenant colonel, and in October he became commander of the regiment that guarded Confederate prisoners at Point Lookout, Maryland, at a post, Adams wrote, "established on a low, sandy, malarious, fever-smitten, wind-blown, God-forsaken tongue of land dividing Chesapeake Bay from the Potomac River."[38] Lieutenant Colonel Adams said about his command:

> By an ingenious move through my influential friends at the Headquarters of the Army of the Potomac, I got the regiment mounted. Mistake number one. The regiment was doing very good service, dismounted, as a garrison and guard over the prisoners' camp at Point Lookout. To mount it, meant only the waste of 1200 much-needed horses. Then, having got it mounted, through the same channels I worked it into active service. Mistake number two; as the only result of so doing was to afford myself convincing proof that the Negro was wholly unfit for cavalry service, lacking absolutely the essential qualities of alertness, individuality, reliability, and self-reliance. He could not scout; he could not take care of himself in unfamiliar positions. The regiment was in exactly its proper place at Point Lookout. I merely took the Negro out of it, and put him where he was of no possible use. I did the service harm, the regiment no good. . . . True, I had the satisfaction of leading my regiment into burning Richmond, the day after Lee abandoned it.[39]

The regiment marched into Richmond on May 20, 1865. Adams, who had been sick for many weeks and weighed only 130 pounds, was brevetted a brigadier general and discharged early in June. Ordered to Clarksville, Texas, a month later,

James T. Wormley mustered out of the army on July 8, 1865, as a sergeant. Colored soldiers, no matter how well they had performed, could not advance into the ranks of commissioned officers until 1865. By the time the war was over only a hundred Negroes, including surgeons and clergymen, had obtained commissions.

Commissioned or not, military service helped change the treatment of Negroes by whites and transformed the way colored people viewed themselves. On the simplest level, large numbers of former slaves learned to read and write. And for the first time in U.S. history, blacks could testify against whites in army courts, and in general were treated as equals, at least before military law. That the impersonal sovereignty of law could supercede the personal authority of the master was a truly revolutionary idea to Negroes. The issue of unequal pay was introduced before Congress because colored soldiers had protested and petitioned for change. Accordingly, Congress in 1864 enacted a measure for equality in pay. In 1865 James T. Wormley and Frederick Douglass's sons, Charles and Lewis, also members of the Fifth Massachusetts Regiment, signed a petition, along with 186 others, asking the secretary of war to allow Negroes to command Negro companies.[40] Once again they succeeded. Not only had colored soldiers played a crucial role in the winning of the Civil War, they helped to accelerate changes in civil rights legislation.

By the time of Wormley's discharge, the Thirteenth Amendment had freed four million slaves, a large portion of them in Washington's bordering states. But what exactly were the former slaves free to do? Largely uneducated and illiterate, they were ill prepared to live on their own. With no surname, they lacked identity. With no property, they came into freedom with nothing but freedom. Facing up to a real emergency, Congress established the Bureau of Refugees, Freedmen, and Abandoned Lands, a temporary agency under the War Department, to assist the emancipated slaves' transition to freedom. Union general Oliver O. Howard, who had lost an arm during the Peninsular Campaign, became its director. Charles Douglass, after an honorable discharge from the Fifth Massachusetts Regiment, went to work for General Howard at a hundred dollars a month and took a room at Wormley's. When white clerks who had been hired before Douglass objected to working with a Negro, Howard stopped their complaints by threatening to fire them and "fill their places with colored men."[41]

James T. Wormley also benefitted from Howard's appointment. After requesting and receiving from Congress a charter to incorporate Howard University,

General Howard set up what eventually became the country's premier black university. Wormley grabbed the chance for a college education, and in 1870 he was the university's first graduate of its medical department with a degree in pharmacy, inspiring his sister, Anna, to pursue a degree in education. After graduation James T. married Mary Ringgold of New Orleans and went to work for a white druggist. Shortly after, the druggist, wanting to retire, agreed to sell his entire stock and equipment to Wormley for thirty-five dollars a month. Using money from the sale of his wife's piano, he procured a year's lease on a location near his brother William's grocery store, his brother Garrett's provisions market, his mother's confectionary, and his father's restaurant, catering establishment, and boarding house, becoming the first member of his race to own a fully equipped pharmacy in Washington.[42] The prosperous Wormleys operated a quasi–I Street monopoly.

Alertness, individuality, reliability, and self-reliance, the qualities Adams had found lacking in his soldiers, were precisely the qualities James Wormley embodied and passed on to his children. Moreover, he was an engaging, affable, polished, shrewd, handsome man, attracting everyone with his piercing black eyes. Francis J. Grimké, the pastor of the Fifteenth Street colored Presbyterian Church called Wormley a "manly man, a man who respected himself and who demanded respect of others. . . . There was nothing obsequious about him in his contact with white people, as so many colored people are."[43] His fame as a caterer of private parties had spread, but it was principally his likeability and dignity that attracted Reverdy Johnson to James Wormley.

Reverdy Johnson, a seventy-two-year-old, half-blind Maryland senator who had for years served on the Senate Foreign Relations Committee, became President Andrew Johnson's appointee to replace the retiring Charles Francis Adams Sr., the father of James T.'s regiment commander, as American minister to Great Britain.[44] The wonder is that President Johnson chose this particular senator, since Reverdy Johnson was the only member of the president's party to break ranks and vote to override his veto of the Reconstruction Act of 1867. This act divided the Confederate states (except Tennessee) into five military districts under commanders empowered to protect life and civil rights, and laid out steps by which new state governments could be created and recognized by Congress. Whatever its flaws, Reverdy Johnson rationalized, the bill offered the South a path back into the Union. He went further—his was the only Democratic vote in favor of the Reconstruction measures of 1866–1867. On the other hand, he had aided in securing acquittal in Andrew Johnson's impeachment proceedings. An outstanding lawyer with an amiable disposition, Reverdy Johnson was easily confirmed, although no one expected much of him. When he presented his credentials to the English court on September 14, 1868, James Wormley accompanied him. Despite his difficulty in transporting live Potomac River terrapin across the ocean and keeping them alive until cooking time, Wormley's culinary diplomacy nicely complemented Reverdy Johnson's success in preparing the way for the peaceful settlement of disputes between England and the United States over the CSS *Alabama* claims. The *Alabama* was the most famous of the Confederate cruisers that preyed on Union ships during the Civil War. Built in England in 1862, the *Alabama* sank, burned, or captured sixty-six Union ships. On the grounds that Great Britain had failed in its obligation of neutrality, the United States demanded payment for damages inflicted by the British-built ship. After Johnson relinquished his charge on May 13, 1869, Wormley went to Paris, purchased dishes and cooking utensils, and returned to Washington in time for the marriage of his niece Marie "Betsey" Wormley, daughter of his brother Andrew, on December 3.

"The Marriage of Paul Gerard and the Pretty Octoroon" headlined the page four story in the Washington *Evening Star*. Friends and family of Presbyterian Miss Wormley and Catholic Paul Gerard of France, a brother-in-law of the Portuguese Minister to Washington, gathered in the parlor of Father White, pastor of St. Matthew's Church, a block from James and Anna Wormley's home. Rumors about the impending wedding had been circulating for weeks because few people believed, according to the *Star*, that a Catholic priest would be allowed to "perform the ceremony marrying a white man and colored woman. In this they were, however, mistaken, as the Catholic Church makes no prohibition on account of race or color."[45] Father White performed the ceremony in English and French, as the groom did not easily understand English. Afterward, the party walked to Andrew Wormley's house on Fourteenth Street, between H and I, for the reception. The couple settled in Paris.

In the new year, between January 17 and December 20, James Wormley borrowed almost $11,000 from the Riggs National Bank in order to open a hotel at 1500 H Street, NW.[46] It is a mark of his repute that among his endorsers was George Riggs, the owner of the bank, and George Robeson, President Grant's secretary of the navy. In 1871 Wormley took out loans totaling nearly $3,900. Finally, with the additional aid of a Republican congressman from Massachusetts, Samuel Hooper, who held the mortgage, he opened Wormley's Hotel in December.

Ideally located in the most fashionable area of the city near Lafayette Square, the White House, and the Treasury and Navy Departments, the building was a five-story structure with seventy-four rooms, including fifty-seven bedrooms, a reception parlor, and large dining, smoking, and wine rooms. All the rooms were big, bright, and handsomely furnished with Brussels carpets and Smyrna rugs. The basement bar and first-class barber shop were always full, and the restaurant soon became Washington's favorite, serving the choicest fowl, fish caught daily in the Chesapeake Bay, meats, and of course Wormley's specialty, terrapin. Wormley's stables, full of horses and carriages for guests' use, occupied the alley behind the hotel. Although Wormley's was the smallest of the city's best hotels, it was the most expensive at five dollars a day, and the most popular, especially with foreigners, partly because Wormley emphasized in person and in his advertisements his unusual ability to provide "European-style" service. He had used his stint with Reverdy Johnson to great advantage.

James Wormley's experience as a hacker, steward, caterer, restaurateur, and boarding house operator laid the groundwork for his success as a hotelier. He had worked hard and carefully tended to his reputation, but his success also took place in the context of expanding rights for Negroes. Because Radical Republicans had political leadership in the city, they used the District of Columbia as a testing ground for national Reconstruction legislation. "Your position is peculiar and more important, for you are placed on a hill, so as to be an example throughout the country," Massachusetts Radical Republican senator Charles Sumner said in an address to city's black population. "Your colored fellow-citizens elsewhere, counted by the millions, will be encouraged or depressed by what is done here."[47] Washington's history in these years, as Sumner's words so accurately foretold, foreshadowed subsequent Southern experiences.

Washington, then, was not only a blueprint for the idea of racial equality, but it became a microcosm of the national urban experience to come. During the Civil War the city's black population was 14,000. By the time Wormley opened his hotel it had surged to well over 40,000, so that Washington had a larger percentage of Negroes than any large city in the nation. Yet despite normal problems attendant upon such a sudden wave of population, black males got the right to vote in 1866, prior to the passage of the Fifteenth Amendment. Thousands registered and voted in the 1867 municipal elections. The city election of 1868 put blacks in local elective office for the first time. In 1871 James Wormley himself served the District in an official capacity. The Supreme Court of the District of

Columbia, pursuant to "an act providing for the selection of Jurors to serve in the several courts of the District of Columbia,"[48] appointed former mayor Sayles J. Bowen; George W. Phillips, the Chief Deputy Marshall of the District; and James Wormley as officers charged with making "lists of Jurors for the service of the Supreme Court."

Beginning in 1869, Washington officials passed a series of public accommodation laws banning the segregation of public facilities like hotels, restaurants, and theaters. Even so, colored educator John F. Cook Jr. was denied a seat at the National Theatre. Wormley spoke out publicly and roused his son James T. and two friends to protest by buying tickets and taking seats in the dress circle. Their ejection was reported in the *Evening Star*, and although never brought to trial, the incident did result in stiffer fines for such discrimination and increased public awareness of nonenforcement of civil rights laws. This awareness in turn prompted the city council to pass additional legislation outlawing discrimination based on race in hotels, taverns, restaurants, and saloons. Although segregation was slowed, not stopped, by similar attempts, life had definitely improved for Negroes in Washington. When Congress allowed public money for "colored schools" in 1862, it gave the secretary of the interior jurisdiction over appointing school board members. In 1870 James Wormley's oldest son, William, was appointed as one of two Negro trustees of the public colored system.[49]

A growing number of black families were buying homes; by 1870 they owned 20 percent of the District's real estate.[50] Negroes also edited a first-rate newspaper, the *New National Era*, which began publishing in 1870 under the coeditorship of Martin Sella, pastor of the Fifteenth Street Presbyterian Church, and Frederick Douglass, one-time slave and abolitionist lecturer who had moved to the District.[51] While its focus was primarily national and it was published only once a week, the paper provided valuable political guidance to blacks. By 1871 Washington seemed to have become the capital for all citizens, black and white.

Wormley, then, opened his hotel against this background of improved legal status for Negroes. And his own status rose considerably, tied as it was to the significant role hotels played in nineteenth-century Washington. The city's hotels functioned as government offices, boarding houses, polling stations, and centers of commercial and financial activity. Even so, Wormley's success depended on his skills as a host, which were so prodigious that Senator Sumner could write Wormley from Cotuit Point on Cape Cod, "I am here for three days with Mr. Hooper [hotel's mortgagor], who read me a letter from Washington saying that you will make out of the hotel $25,000 the first year. Good! Three cheers!"[52]

In 1872, when the average federal employee made $1,000 a year, $25,000 was big money indeed.

GRANT'S SECOND ADMINISTRATION AND NEEDED REFORM

*A*s James Wormley celebrated his first year running Wormley's Hotel, Ulysses S. Grant handily won a second term as president, carrying 56 percent of the popular vote despite a serious split within his party.[1] Grant had tarnished his image as a resourceful Civil War leader by his indifference toward civil service reform, a proclivity for appointing military cronies and relatives to executive branch positions, and an imperturbability toward the political indiscretions—and worse—of his handpicked advisers.

Hints of restiveness among Republicans began to surface as early as the 1870 congressional campaign, when Vice President Schuyler Colfax announced that he would retire from political life at the end of Grant's first term. Washingtonians wondered why. Colfax had been an extremely well-liked Speaker of the House, and he was only fifty years old. Was Colfax quitting because he chafed at the way Grant wasted most of his time on appointments to unimportant offices, ignoring larger issues? When many of Colfax's friends started criticizing Grant publicly, rumor had it that Colfax yearned for the top spot. Not so, said the vice president.

By early 1872 the critics bolted to form a new party, the Liberal Republicans. An impressive group of men aligned themselves in the revolt against Grant—men like Salmon P. Chase, Lincoln's secretary of the treasury and Supreme Court justice; Gideon Welles, President Lincoln's and President Johnson's secretary of the navy; William Cullen Bryant, poet and editor of the *New York Evening Post*; Jacob

D. Cox, Grant's first secretary of the interior, who had earlier resigned over a policy dispute with the president; Montgomery Blair, Lincoln's first postmaster general; Charles Sumner, senator from Massachusetts; Carl Schurz, journalist and Missouri senator; Charles Francis Adams, Lincoln's hugely successful Civil War minister to England and the father of the Charles Adams who had commanded James T. Wormley's regiment; and Lyman Trumbull, senator from Illinois. Had any one of these men been nominated to run against Grant, the result would never have been such a rout. In choosing as their candidate the *New York Tribune* editor Horace Greeley, however, they all but guaranteed a big loss. Greeley had at first called for general amnesty for the South combined with the assurance of civil rights for the Negro. But to get the nomination he dropped the civil rights condition. Most abolitionists, black and white, remained loyal to the president because they believed his Southern policy offered better protection for the Negro. Although the Liberal Republican and Democratic platforms affirmed the Reconstruction amendments, most antislavery people discerned grave danger for the Negro in their program of conciliation to, and self-government for, Southerners. Greeley, after all, was on record as saying that continued federal interference in the South would drive all Southern whites into the Democratic Party and intensify anti-Negro terrorism, which by 1872 was considerable all over the South. Most abolitionists and the thousands of whites who had gone to the South to help the freedmen saw this terrorism up close. They believed a Liberal victory would spell disaster for the Negro. Only by an uncompromising enforcement of the law could the conditions for equality be created. Self-government for the states amounted to state sovereignty, the very cause for which the rebels fought.

The election gave James Wormley a lot to ponder. He knew only too well how anti-Grant his friend and neighbor Charles Sumner was, as Sumner had made it clear since March that he could not support the president. After the regular Republicans at Philadelphia renominated Grant by acclamation, Sumner decided to sit out the presidential campaign in silence. On July 11, 1872, however, a group of prominent Washington Negroes—Wormley's oldest son, William, among them— wrote a letter to Sumner requesting his opinion of the candidates.[2] His public reply on July 29 revealed how ambivalent he felt about Greeley, but in the end Sumner threw in his lot with the Liberal Republicans, albeit very reluctantly and only because of personal and political difficulties with the president. He considered the federal government's protection of civil rights the paramount issue of the day, just as he had regarded the abolition of slavery as the preeminent problem of the pre-war era, and he regretted Greeley's naive faith in the good will of Southern states'-rights whites to respect Negroes' newly won civil rights.

Making electoral matters muddier for Wormley, Schuyler Colfax changed his mind about the vice presidency and opened a headquarters in Wormley's Hotel for the purpose of attaining a renomination. Grant, however, had already let it be known that he supported the "other" senator from Massachusetts, Henry Wilson. "The revocation of the Vice President of his declination was to me a surprise," Wilson said, "but [I am] not withdrawing from the contest."[3] The convention chose Wilson.

In the fall heat of the campaign the *New York Sun* published a sensational story about the creation in the 1860s of a construction company called Crédit Mobilier, put together to help finance the Union Pacific Railroad in a fashion highly profitable to a few inside men. The federal government had subsidized the Union Pacific to construct a road by a central route westward to meet the Central Pacific Railroad, building east from San Francisco. Because insiders feared regulation, they gave Massachusetts representative Oakes Ames 343 shares of Crédit Mobilier to distribute to key congressmen. Not until after the election, in December 1872, were these congressmen identified. Among the beneficiaries in the House were Speaker James Blaine; Henry Dawes, chairman of the Ways and Means Committee; and James Garfield, chairman of the Appropriations Committee, all Republicans and all-powerful House members. Both vice presidents, outgoing Schuyler Colfax and the incoming Henry Wilson, and various other senators and representatives—twenty in all—were implicated. All were Republicans except for James Brooks, a Democratic representative from New York. Only Ames, who committed the unforgivable sin of naming names, and Brooks, the lone Democrat, were condemned by Congress. Even so, the Republican whitewash of their fellows did not go unnoticed in the press.

In March, only a few months after the censure of Brooks and Ames, the Republican majority—the party controlled Congress by a two-thirds margin—led by Ben Butler of Massachusetts introduced and passed the Salary Bill of 1873, ever after referred to as the "Salary Grab Act." The act doubled the president's salary; cabinet officers and Supreme Court justices got handsome raises; and members of Congress voted themselves a 50 percent increase to $7,500 a year, this to be retroactive for two years, thereby giving each member a $5,000 gift as well as a 50 percent raise. The public started calling the act the "back-pay" steal. Making this matter worse in the public's mind was the financial panic of 1873, which led to the longest depression hitherto sustained by the United States. Without liberal critics, those who had split from the party in 1872, whatever official rectitude remained within the administration collapsed, and Democrats reaped the harvest. In the 1874 off-year election they regained control of the House of Representatives for the first time since secession.

Senator Charles Sumner returned his salary "gift" to the treasury. Exactly one year later one of the best congressional friends Negroes had ever had was dead. On the night of March 10, 1874, as he worked in his study, Sumner fell heavily to the floor. Servants summoned James Wormley from his hotel around the corner. With his help they lifted Sumner to the bed, where he lingered for a painful fourteen hours. Wormley remained at his bedside the whole time. Doctors, friends, and colleagues called on Sumner for brief visits. Representative Samuel Hooper, who lived next door, looked in on the patient off and on throughout the night, reassured by Wormley's solicitude. Not only did Hooper hold the mortgage on Wormley's hotel, his widowed daughter-in-law, Alice Mason Hooper, had married Sumner in October of 1866, after Representative Hooper's son died in 1863. They did not officially divorce until 1873, although they separated only months after the marriage.[4] When Frederick Douglass came to the sickroom, Sumner repeated his injunction, "my bill, the civil-rights bill, don't let it fail."[5] Negroes gathered outside his house on Vermont Avenue and H Street, just across Lafayette Park from the White House. By midday the streets were jammed. At two p.m. he died.

Two days later his coffin sat in the rotunda of the Capitol on the same black catafalque where Lincoln's body had lain. This was the first time in American history a senator had been so honored. That afternoon Grant and his cabinet, the justices of the Supreme Court, members of the diplomatic corps, and members of the House and Senate watched as Sumner's coffin was brought into the Senate chamber. After the service, delegations from both houses accompanied the body on a special funeral train to Massachusetts. The next day, March 15, the coffin lay in state in the State House in Boston. A shield with the words "Don't Let the Civil Rights Bill Die" covered the top of the casket. The pallbearers—literary greats Ralph Waldo Emerson, John Greenleaf Whittier, Henry Wadsworth Longfellow; politicos Robert Winthrop and Charles Francis Adams; and five former governors—escorted the casket the five-mile route from the State House to King's Chapel for the funeral, and to Mount Auburn for internment. Mourners quietly lined the streets the entire way.

Newspapers across the country eulogized Sumner's political life and, given the endless appetite for oratory during the nineteenth century, audiences assembled everywhere to hear the senator extolled. Over and over they listened to stories about Sumner's break with the Whig party over the annexation of Texas and recalled how he had joined with other anti-slavery men to form the Free Soil party. They learned about Sumner's first election to the Senate in 1851 and of his allegiance to the tiny anti-slavery minority in Congress. They relived Sumner's ferocious 1856 beating on the floor of the Senate by Representative Preston Brooks, a South Carolinian enraged by Sumner's anti-slavery orations, and how it took three years for Sumner to recover from his wounds. On and on the tributes went, but no one heard a word about what legislation Sumner had gotten passed. The fact was, that after nearly a quarter of a century in the Senate, Sumner had been instrumental in the adoption of very few laws, or, as his fellow Massachusetts senator George Boutwell said, somewhat humorously, only one law: a statute permitting Mongolian immigrants to be naturalized.[6] Although an impractical idealist, Sumner did get Congress to pass legislation banning segregated cars on all street railways in Washington as early as 1865, but streetcars did not include intercity railroads. When the Washington, Georgetown, and Alexandria Railroad discriminated against Mrs. Kate Brown, who worked in the ladies room in the Senate wing of the Capitol, Sumner fought for her rights on the Senate floor on February 11, 1868. When the Senate took no action, two Negro men, one of whom was Mrs. Brown's brother, took the same train from the city across the Long Bridge into Alexandria. Once again the conductor insisted they ride in a car for blacks. When they refused, they were ejected. Mrs. Brown sued, alleging violation of the Civil Rights Act of 1866. The case went all the way to the United States Supreme Court where she secured a favorable decision in 1873.[7]

Sumner was, of course, the leading proponent of Negro rights in the Senate, yet he had neither written nor sponsored nor approved of the Thirteenth, Fourteenth, or Fifteenth Amendments. But he was exactly what his Massachusetts supporters wanted him to be and that was "the embodiment of the moral idea, with all its uncompromising firmness," as Carl Schurz put it.[8] No acting was necessary for him to play the part of "statesman doctrinaire," as Charles Francis Adams said. A person who is principle personified will not have any truck with compromise. But compromise is necessary to get legislation passed.

President Grant had attended Sumner's Capitol funeral only for appearances. He so disliked the Massachusetts senator he had gotten him expelled from the chairmanship of the Foreign Relations Committee at the end of 1871, and he never supported the civil rights bill, the passage of which had been Sumner's foremost goal. But in May 1872 the president's congressional supporters suddenly realized that if no civil rights legislation was passed, Sumner might use the issue to influence the Negro vote, which had been staunchly pro-Grant in the 1868 election. In fact, the addition of Negroes to the electorate was crucial in Ulysses S. Grant's slim 300,000-vote margin of victory over Horatio Seymour. Thus Wisconsin senator Matthew Carpenter introduced and got passed a weakened version of the bill. It contained no provision to prevent racial discrimination in selecting juries, did not outlaw segregated schools, and kept all civil rights enforcement with the state courts, amounting in fact to no enforcement in the South.

Sumner reacted with a last attempt to persuade his party to reject Grant's leadership. On May 31 he delivered a four-hour oration titled "Republicanism versus Grantism." Among other charges, Sumner called Grant "radically unfit for Presidential office," as he was "first in nepotism, first in gift-taking and repaying by official patronage . . . now rich in houses, lands, and stock." Moreover, he was guilty of an "ostentatious assumption of Infallibility," thereby enabling him to ignore the advice of anyone about almost everything. As a result, his presidency was "an enormous failure."[9]

No matter—Grant won reelection and Sumner spent his last two senatorial years on the outs, so much so that a full year elapsed after his death before the supplemental civil rights act became law. "An act to protect all citizens in Civil and Legal Rights," it guaranteed equal treatment in all places of public accommodation to "all persons within the jurisdiction of the U.S." regardless of "nativity, race, color, or persuasion religious or political."

Not until December 1875, when the newly elected Democratic House of Representatives convened its first session—it was a peculiarity of nineteenth-century politics that more than a year elapsed between the election of Congress and its initial meeting—were Sumner's charges fully corroborated. The 44th Congress had been elected on claims of pervasive corruption within the Grant administration, and the newly elected members were eager to demonstrate the validity of their claims. The task posed little difficulty. Before they had finished, they had investigated every one of Grant's departments, and all, even squeaky-clean Secretary of State Hamilton Fish's Department of State, were found wanting, yet it would be Robert Schenck's slipperiness, a Grant appointee and not a Fish pick, who besmirched State.

Grant's advisers, for the most part, consisted of army cronies from the war, and Robert Schenck, a Civil War general, was one of them. After he lost his congressional seat in the House (Ohio), Grant made him minister to Great Britain. Once in London, still the center of capital investment not only for the entire British Empire but for the United States as well, Schenck lost no time exploiting his position, with its connections, for his own financial well-being. Although the minister knew nothing about silver or silver mining, when the Emma Mines, a Utah silver holding company, was organized in England, he lent his name as director in return for $2,500 in annual salary and $10,000 worth of stock in his name, for one year with guaranteed dividends. If the stock fell, he could surrender his block without loss; if it rose, he kept the profit. Moreover, Schenck enthusiastically endorsed the stock in newspaper advertisements. A horrified Hamilton Fish told the minister to withdraw his name from the prospectus and advertisements, which Schenck did, but only after a six-week delay to give him and his friends time to sell their stock before the market fell. Exposure brought the minister home in disgrace.

Even before Schenck's ignominy, Treasury Secretary William A. Richardson had to be let go for appointing John D. Sanborn as special agent for collecting delinquent taxes and letting him retain a whopping 50 percent of all revenue collected. A House investigation revealed that Sanborn had collected more than $400,000 in back taxes, half of which he kept. An honest Kentuckian, William Bristow, succeeded Richardson at Treasury.

Next to go was Attorney General George Williams. After two years of allegations claiming that he had blocked investigations that could have embarrassed him, that he accepted bribes, and that he used Justice Department money to pay for his wife's extravagances, new evidence surfaced in 1875 that both he and his wife had demanded money from businesses to drop suits before the Justice Department. Threatened with impeachment, he resigned.

Interior Secretary Columbus Delano, it was discovered, had been awarding his son John and Grant's brother Orvil partnerships in surveying contracts that surveyors would not otherwise have received, even though neither John nor Orvil ever rendered cartographical service. Secretary of State Fish and Treasury Secretary Benjamin Bristow, the sole unblemished cabinet members, told Grant to demand Delano's resignation, but Grant refused. When pressure mounted owing to extensive newspaper coverage, Grant told Delano he had to go but then did not announce his decision for several months. In October 1875 Zachariah Chandler, Grant's old friend from his army days in Detroit, took Delano's place as Secretary of the Interior.

Secretary of the Navy George Robeson, who had in 1871 cosigned a bank loan with James Wormley, formed a business connection with a grain firm in Philadelphia named A. G. Catell and Company. Although the Catells had never dealt with the navy or with any other governmental agency before Robeson's elevation to navy secretary, after Robeson nearly all their contracts were to supply foodstuffs to the navy. Small wonder that Robeson—who on an $8,000 annual salary and net worth of $20,000 managed to deposit $320,000 in his bank account—prospered. Congressional investigators accused the secretary of gross misconduct, and although there was some talk of impeachment, other scandals rose to the fore and the Robeson matter disappeared.

Seemingly undismayed by and at times even uninterested in the mounting scandals, Grant came to complete attention when Treasury Secretary Benjamin Bristow discovered Orville Babcock's involvement in the whiskey frauds. Babcock, Grant's personal secretary, chief assistant, and close friend, was another of the president's war cronies, an unexceptional man whom Grant had met during the Chattanooga campaign and whom he later appointed to his staff. Babcock was convivial, yet shrewd in never questioning Grant and in having a knack for articulating his commander's enthusiasms.

In late 1875 Bristow uncovered a conspiracy of hundreds of distillers and federal officials who were diverting millions of dollars in liquor taxes into their own pockets. At first Grant called for swift retribution, even after he learned that John McDonald, yet another war buddy, was the central figure in the fraud. Grant had appointed General McDonald of St. Louis to be collector of internal revenue for the district, which included seven states, and in return McDonald lavishly entertained the presidential party on an 1874 visit to St. Louis, presenting his commander with two fine horses. When confronted with Bristow's evidence, McDonald confessed. The grand jury in St. Louis returned 253 indictments against McDonald, who later went to jail.

In the meantime whiskey ring prosecutions went forward in Milwaukee, Chicago, and several smaller cities. Newspapers in January 1876 suggested that Grant's brother Orvil, his brother-in-law Lewis Dent (who had died in 1874), and his oldest son, Fred, had been getting whiskey money. In all, 110 conspirators were convicted. Babcock's trial was scheduled to open in February in St. Louis. Until that time Babcock and his close friend, Secretary of War William Belknap—the cabal, as Hamilton Fish referred to them—labored night and day to fill Grant's mind with distrust of the whiskey ring prosecutions. Their success is evidenced by Grant's growing dislike and mistrust of Bristow, and his determination to go to St. Louis as a character witness for Babcock. With great difficulty Fish managed to persuade the president that to try to protect a man arrested for a crime was not only unprecedented, it was also a terrible idea. Grant compromised by being deposed by defense lawyers at the White House. Even so, a sitting president had never before, and has not since, testified voluntarily as a defense witness in a criminal trial.[10] Babcock's chief defense attorney, Emory Storrs, brazenly said otherwise in his closing argument: "Grant was no volunteer witness, but was fortunately called by the exigencies of the case."[11] Grant's deposition and Storrs's untruthfulness achieved Babcock's acquittal, which came on February 28, 1876. Of all the major St. Louis Whiskey Ring defendants, Babcock alone won acquittal.[12] Babcock returned to Washington and showed up at the White House for work, and there he probably would have remained for the rest of the administration's tenure if Fish had not insisted he had to go. Grant replaced him with his son Buck and rewarded his friend with a sinecure—inspector of lighthouses.

News stories of the cumulative treachery of his cabinet and advisers seemed to roll off Grant until the Belknap Affair. On February 29, the day after Babcock's acquittal made national headlines, the House Committee on Expenditures in the War Department called its first witness, Caleb Marsh, in the emerging post-tradership scandal. The U.S. Army operated stores for its military personnel and their families as well as authorized civilians at military camps. Since the secretary of war had jurisdiction over the traders who ran the combination general store-saloons at frontier military posts, and since Marsh's testimony directly implicated Belknap in a kickback scheme, Hiester Clymer, committee chairman and former Princeton classmate of the secretary of war, invited him to attend a committee meeting at 10:30 a.m. on March 1. Belknap appeared; Clymer read aloud Marsh's comments. As the war secretary asked to employ counsel, the committee adjourned until three p.m. When Belknap reappeared with his lawyer, Clymer reread Marsh's testimony.

The next morning, March 2, a disheveled and distraught William Belknap, accompanied by Interior Secretary Zachariah Chandler, called on President Grant as he was leaving for a studio sitting with portrait painter Henry Ulke, the same painter James Wormley had commissioned to do oil portraits for his hotel. "Belknap was changed so you would hardly know him," Grant later related. "He looked as if he had not slept in a week."[13] The cabinet secretary broke down when he saw the president. Weeping, he told Grant "in an incoherent way about the congressional investigation." He begged his chief to accept his immediate resignation, which he had already put in writing. With little pause, Grant stood at the mantel and wrote, "Your tender of resignation as Secretary of War, with the request to have it accepted immediately, is received and the same is hereby accepted with great regret." With acceptance in hand, Belknap and Chandler hurried to deliver Grant's words to Belknap's lawyer who presented them to Clymer's committee at 11:30 a.m. At three that afternoon the committee submitted a report "that they had found at the very threshold of their investigation such unquestioned evidence of malfeasance in office by General Belknap" that duty required them to recommend he be impeached.[14]

Under the Constitution the House impeaches and the Senate tries the impeachment. On April 3 the House submitted to the Senate the articles of impeachment. Three days later the sergeant-at-arms of the Senate served a summons on Belknap.

As the trial began during the Easter season, the galleries were crowded with ladies in their Easter bonnets. By the time the proceedings ended late in July, the galleries were still full despite the nearly unbearable Washington summer heat and humidity. The trial ended with Belknap's acquittal, not because he was innocent but because enough senators bought the technical contention that when the House voted for impeachment, Belknap had already resigned; hence, the "Senate was under the Constitution without jurisdiction."[15]

Anyone who reads the 1,122 printed pages of the testimony of 50 witnesses comes to the unequivocal conclusion that Belknap had built up an almost foolproof system of patronage that brought financial benefits to himself and to his and Grant's friends and relatives. The specific charge under indictment concerned the relationship between Belknap and Marsh in relation to the Fort Sill trader post.

On August 16, 1870, Caleb Marsh, a New York furniture manufacturer and tea importer, applied for appointment as post trader at Fort Sill, Indian Territory. Marsh was a friend of Belknap. But Fort Sill already had a post trader, a John Evans, who had a large investment in the post store and who was enthusiastically recommended for reappointment by the commandant and officers at the fort. Not to be reappointed would mean financial disaster, as Evans had his money tied up in the buildings at the fort as well as in supplies.

To plead his case, Evans went to Washington and paid General Rice, another of Belknap's friends, $1,000 to see the secretary of war for him.[16] Learning that Belknap was in Keokuk, Iowa, Evans traveled there only to be rebuffed by the war secretary, who told him to return to Washington and wait there to conduct business. Despite all Evans's attempts, Marsh, with no recommendations on file, got the appointment. To save what he could of his investment at Fort Sill, Evans entered into a contract with Marsh on October 8, 1870, according to which Evans was to remain post trader as the appointee of Marsh and in return was to pay his "benefactor" $12,000 annually, half of which extortion Marsh paid to Belknap. On the same day as signing the contract, Marsh wrote to Belknap: "I have to ask that the appointment which you have given me . . . be made in the name of Evans, as it will be more convenient for me to have him manage the business at present."[17] Before 1870 that sort of cupidity could never have happened, but on July 15, 1870, Congress passed a law that authorized the secretary of war alone to control the appointment and removal of traders stationed on army reservations. Before the 1870 law the officers of military posts supervised traders so that prices could not get too far out of line. With the new system, post traderships became political plums to be given to heavy party contributors or to friends and relatives. Although Marsh lived in New York, and never invested a cent in the post, he got $12,000 a year for having the good fortune to know the secretary of war. The extra expense such arrangements necessitated—the post trader raised prices to pay for his privilege of trading—came out of the pockets of the post's soldiers, already poorly paid, and Indians, most near poverty. Furthermore, since the law only permitted one trader per post, competition was effectively stifled.

Between 1870 and 1876 Evans paid Marsh $42,317.02; Marsh paid Belknap $24,450. Testimony from Adams Express Company agents (Marsh often sent his remittance to Belknap via Adams Express), from the chief clerk of the War Department, and of the bookkeeper and cashier of the New York bank where the original certificates of deposit from Marsh to Belknap were filed, proved beyond doubt the accuracy and reality of the transactions. Deposit slips and bank accounts showing deposits and withdrawals by Belknap, or his clerk for him, were also produced. Marsh's and Evans's testimony went unchallenged; Belknap never took the stand.

Facing irrefutable evidence of their client's guilt, Belknap's lawyers relied on character witnesses and non sequiturs to distract, disarm, and discomfit the offense. "These articles of impeachment were served upon General Belknap at 5:40 in the afternoon of April 6, 1876," began one such non sequitur.[18] "On April 6, 1862, at about the same hour, General Belknap was in the forefront of the line of Union troops who made their last stand and rolled back the Confederate forces on the bloody field of Shiloh." Character witnesses like generals John Pope, Christopher Augur, Thomas Ruger, Andrew Humphreys, and Winfield Scott

Hancock; Gov. Ralph Lowe and Sen. William Allison of Iowa; and Judge Samuel Miller of the U.S. Supreme Court vouched for Belknap's integrity.

Although the impeachment managers failed to obtain the necessary two-thirds vote, and although Belknap escaped criminal prosecution, he was ever after a marked man. The Belknap acquittal came in August 1876, only three months before the presidential election. It seems odd that this scandal, piddling compared to the whiskey frauds and Crédit Mobilier affairs, should have dealt the president such a devastating blow. At long last, Vice President Wilson's January 1875 warning to Rep. James Garfield had come to pass: "Grant is now more unpopular than Andrew Johnson was in his darkest days; . . . [yet] Grant is still struggling for a third term; in short . . . he is a millstone around the neck of our party that would sink it out of sight."[19]

Grant and his wife, Julia, did indeed want a third term. The White House was their home and an oasis in a world in which they never felt at home. "My life at the White House was like a bright and beautiful dream and we were immeasurably happy," Julia Grant wrote of her eight years there, the longest period she and Ulysses lived together anywhere in their married life.[20] Grant wanted a third term because, quite simply, he was prepared to do nothing else. The White House offered security and a seemingly loyal staff. The Belknap affair dashed all such hopes. As President Grant's second administration had fallen apart in a storm of scandal, the winds of reform gathered force. It would be the issue of the coming presidential election. Accordingly, Republicans set about finding a more acceptable nominee. House Democrats had forced the nation's attention on the corruption of the Grant administration knowing they already had a reform candidate.

Not only had the Democrats retaken the House of Representatives in the 1874 election—they elected one hundred new congressmen—they had also won key gubernatorial races in the five Northern states of Connecticut, Massachusetts, New York, Pennsylvania, and Ohio, the most important being New York. As the new governor of the Empire State, Samuel Jones Tilden became overnight a national figure. His timing could not have been better. Elected because he successfully prosecuted the notorious William "Boss" Tweed Ring that had stolen millions from the city of New York—estimates range from $20 million to over $200 million—his reform image exactly fit the mood of a country angered by the steady drumbeat of scandals issuing forth from Washington.

Tilden had grown up in New Lebanon, a small town near Albany. As the son of a local party leader, he was nurtured on the conversations of his father's Democratic friends. New York governor and future president Martin Van Buren made the biggest impression on the young boy. After schooling, Tilden went on to become one of the nation's most sought-after railroad lawyers, amassing a fortune through his practice, yet all the while active in local politics. Slender, sickly, smart, shrewd, and a man of unquestioned integrity, he was a strange creature to have gone so far in politics. He was the soul of indecision and procrastination, often secretive and always hypochondriacal. Even so, he elicited trust and inspired younger men to enter politics. Despite his bachelorhood and innate lack of sociability, the sixty-year-old, who lived among fine art objects, classical books, a stupendous collection of pornography, and imported wines in an elegant Gramercy Park townhouse, did entertain intimates on occasion. Even then he was aloof, but as annoying as his aloofness could be, what seemed to matter to the public was his willingness to put everything on the line to root out endemic corruption. This carried him far in a profession that regularly rewarded gregarious gladhanders.

Both Samuel Tilden and William Tweed belonged to Tammany Hall, New York City's powerful Democratic political machine. The word Tammany comes from Tamanend, a Delaware Indian chief well known and well liked in the early colonial period. Tammany Hall was founded after the Revolution as a fraternal society for former enlisted soldiers, a rank-and-file counterpart to the Cincinnatus Society, the fraternal organization for General Washington's officers. William Tweed became the Hall's most powerful boss.

Tweed was Tilden's opposite in nearly every way: warm-hearted, outgoing, massive in size—at his prime he weighed close to three hundred pounds—and generous, especially in helping the underdog. The personification of urban corruption, he and his cohorts stole millions from city and state coffers to enrich themselves, as well as to provide for poor immigrants and for people down on their luck—in return for votes. Tweed got his break in machine politics when he was appointed deputy street commissioner in 1863, a job that enabled him to make deals with contractors who supplied road-building materials to the city. To get city jobs, contractors had to pad their bills by 35 percent. Tweed kept 25 percent of the extortion for his family and his considerable charities, and paid 10 percent to various cronies, thereby creating a ring, a conspiratorial cabal within the Hall. He placed these cohorts in key city posts.

Next Tweed enlisted powerful allies in the judiciary, including three judges, so that the ring would not have to worry about prosecution. In 1868 he went to the legislature as a state senator at the same time his protégé, New York mayor John

Hoffman, captured the governorship. Tammany's forces, marshaled by Tweed, proposed a new city charter that would restore home rule to the metropolis, thereby returning power over the police force, the city's health, fire prevention, education, public works, charities, buildings, and docks to the city, and by extension, Tweed. Moreover, the charter made all department heads mayoral appointments and required the Common Council to muster a three-fourths vote on all bills involving expenditures. At the same time the charter allowed the city virtually unlimited borrowing for improvements. To get the charter passed cost Tweed, by his own account, $600,000 in bribes, most of it going, he groused, to Republicans and their party coffers.[21] The price was small, since it cleared the way for the trio of Tweed and his comrades Mayor Abraham Oakey Hall and Comptroller Richard Connolly to control city finances.

Tweed presided over the Department of Public Works, a consolidation of the former Street Department and Croton Aqueduct Board, a sewerage and water board. He authorized miles of sewer, water, and gas pipelines and appointed knowledgeable people to oversee the enterprise. Then he started in on roads. Over a thousand men in the pay of Tweed's department bid out miles of hundred-foot-wide macadamized avenues and fifty-foot-wide streets with key cross-town connectors at Fifty-seventh, Seventy-ninth, and Eighty-sixth Streets. Tweed also fostered development by leasing out or giving away land to hospitals, schools, and museums. Overall Tweed did a great job improving the city's infrastructure, albeit with padded contracts that inflated construction costs. Public taxes increased from under $10 million in 1860 to $23 million in 1870,[22] and the public debt tripled, from $30 million in 1867 to $90 million in 1871.[23]

Although lavish in his contributions to charity and to the needy and in his entertaining at his Fifth Avenue mansion at Forty-third Street; at his Greenwich, Connecticut, country house; and on his two steam-powered yachts, he stewed about what people thought. Seeking to mold public opinion, he cultivated newspaper editors, gave lucrative jobs to reporters, and used advertising contracts as bribes. He bought controlling interest in a printing company. Before long the Boss's company did all the city's official printing at inflated rates. Tweed also advised officers of railroads, ferries, and insurance companies to use his printing services lest the city curtail their business. The ultimate symbol of Tweed's misdeeds was the New York City County Courthouse at 52 Chambers Street, opposite City Hall in Lower Manhattan. In 1858 the city appropriated $250,000 for a building designed by architect John Kellum. Not until 1862, when Tweed took charge, did construction begin. During the next nine years $13 million of city money went to building and furnishing the small, three-story, barely one-hundred-foot-tall courthouse, and still it was unfinished. This extravagant and brazen graftmanship—just the bill for plastering the iron and marble building came to $2,871,464 plus $1,294,685 to repair the new plaster—finally galvanized honest New Yorkers into action.[24]

In the fall of 1870 the *New York Times* began a campaign against the ring. Long on invective and short on facts, the series of stories pressured Mayor Hall to summon a blue ribbon panel of six businessmen, including Jacob Astor. He gave them access to municipal accounts; by the end of the year the group declared the accounts in order and Tweed's policies and debt levels manageable. The *Times* continued anyway, by this time with more solid evidence provided by a disgruntled insider. Offered a considerable sum to stop, the paper's editor kept on. In retaliation Tweed ordered city officials to boycott the restaurant under the *Times* building, not to pay the $13,764 the city owed the paper, and to confiscate the *Times* on trumped-up title defects. Tweed himself felt more intimidated by cartoonist Thomas Nast of *Harper's Weekly* than by the *New York Times*. Nast's cartoons, he was sure, were contributing to his growing troubles. He sent a banker to offer Nast a half a million to take a long trip to Europe. This also failed.

By now the ever-cautious Tilden was ready to act. Because Tweed controlled votes, Tilden had worked with him to get Democrats elected to office. Never prying too closely into Tweed's methods nor realizing how corrupt his fellow Tammany colleague really was, Tilden, by late 1870, could ignore the Boss's misdeeds no longer, and he took on the uneasy role of civic reformer. His opportunity occurred when the mayor tried to get city comptroller Connolly to resign. The treasurer suspected, rightfully enough, that he was being set up as the ring's scapegoat. He went to Tilden for legal advice. Tilden advised him not to resign and to appoint a deputy of Tilden's choice with custody of all documents. Connolly hoped that by following Tilden's advice he might escape what more and more looked like impending indictment. Tilden's own law associate and friend Andrew Green was sworn in as Connolly's deputy. Green obtained the city's accounts in the National Broadway Bank. Tilden and two assistants devoted ten long days to going over the figures, and showed that Tweed had received 24 percent of all money collected from the city by contractor Andrew Garvey, and 42 percent of all money collected by contractor James H. Ingersoll, whose bills totaled almost $6.5 million.[25]

When the state Democratic Convention assembled in Rochester on October 4, 1871, chairman Samuel Tilden called it to order. Castigating the ring and the "partnership of plunder between men of both parties," he issued a battle cry for action in the coming election.[26] He made no mention of the Council of Political Reform, later renamed the Committee of Seventy, which had been agitating reform for more than a year. Nevertheless, Tilden took over the reform movement begun by the *New York Times*'s stories and urged the election of reform candidates. Tilden was heard: machine candidates suffered landslide losses. Only Tweed returned to Albany. The day after the election Hamilton Fish wrote Tilden: "An old personal friend, whose views on political questions have generally differed from yours, thanks you from the bottom of his heart for your noble work."[27]

For the next sixteen months, Tilden, to the detriment of his own law practice, worked tirelessly. He studied records, gave testimony, argued against appeals, drew up briefs, and advised and directed the legal charge against Boss Tweed and the ring. As part of his effort to get at the ring, Tilden himself ran for the legislature as assemblyman in the eighteenth district of New York County. From January 3 until May 4, 1872, he attended legislative sessions and succeeded in removing Tweed judges; two were impeached and one resigned. But it was the accumulation of evidence that sent Tweed to jail in 1873. Although sentenced to twelve years, he was released after a year on a technicality. Rearrested on a separate charge and retried, he returned to jail. Tweed escaped on December 4, 1875, and fled to Cuba and thence to Spain, where he was recognized and returned to New York. Back in the Ludlow Street jail in late 1876, he died in prison at age fifty-five.

By 1874 Tilden was clearly the frontrunner in the gubernatorial race. Elected as a reform governor, he did nothing to disappoint. Right away he busied himself in an effort to overthrow yet another corrupt ring, the Canal Ring. Members of both political parties had accumulated fortunes by submitting highly inflated bills for repairing the upstate Erie Canal. Although many of the thieves were themselves legislators, they did not dare vote against a resolution authorizing the governor to appoint a Commission of Investigation. As a result the frauds stopped, service on the canal improved, and the state saved millions. By 1876 Tilden was the man of the hour, a hero greatly admired all over the country. Once again his timing was superb, as his rising star coincided with the clear resurgence of his party.

IN THE BLINK
OF AN EYE

*L*ike New York, the nation's capital had a political boss. Unlike Boss Tweed, who used his political power to abscond with municipal funds and fashion an unofficial welfare system for the poor as well as himself and his cronies, Alexander Shepherd, born in Washington in 1836, used his political clout to turn the "city of magnificent intentions" that Charles Dickens had ridiculed into an actual magnificent city—in the staggeringly short period of three years. Shepherd ordered old buildings torn down, railroad tracks torn up, streets widened and paved, sidewalks graded and lit, sewers buried, mosquito-infested canals filled in, aqueducts dug, and parks created. Boss Shepherd represented a new breed that was becoming increasingly common throughout Northern Republican circles—the businessman-politician. His goal in rejuvenating Washington was to make it the trade center its founders had envisioned. That in transforming the city at lightning speed he ran up enormous debt is not surprising. What is unusual is that unprecedented municipal power devolved upon one individual. How did it happen?

By the early 1870s the Negro population in Boss Shepherd's native town had reached 44,000. By then Congress had chartered Howard University, passed a bill guaranteeing unrestricted male suffrage in the District, and had gotten the passage of the Fourteenth Amendment, which guaranteed equal protection of laws to all citizens. Washington's city council passed civil rights measures barring discrimination in hotels, restaurants, bars, and other places of public entertainment. Life had definitely improved for people of color, but the city as a whole was an economic mess. Many whites not only felt that the city's social revolution had gone too far, too fast, but that it should never have been initiated in the first place. They blamed Sayles Bowen, the Radical Republican mayor who had presided over the city from 1868 to 1870, the period that saw the biggest gains in social legislation. Opposition Republicans, the conservatives, united with Democrats in 1870 to put together a "reform" ticket headed by Matthew Emery. The city's fiscal problems did not improve under Emery. Never taking into account its responsibilities as the city's largest landlord, Congress blamed all of Washington's citizens for its precarious monetary situation. So in February 1871 Congress scrapped the city's fifty-one-year-old charter.

Since May 15, 1820, Washington City had popularly elected its mayors, its eight-member board of aldermen, and twelve-member board of common council biennially. In granting the city local government, Congress had made it clear it wanted nothing to do with its finances. Police, fire, streets, sewerage, feeding the poor, educating the young—all had to be financed by Washington's permanent inhabitants. That changed in 1871 when Georgetown, Washington City (the area between the capitol and the White House), and Washington County were merged into a territorial form of government. Alexandria had retroceded to Virginia in 1846. Henceforth, Washington would be administered by a governor and an eleven-member governor's council, appointed by the president and ratified by the Senate, and by a twenty-two-member House of Delegates; a nonvoting delegate to the House of Representatives would also be elected. In addition, an appointed Board of Health and a five-man Board of Public Works would take charge of public improvements and fix property assessments and/or issue bonds to meet the cost of their improvements.

Residents complained about the bill's having vested too much authority in non-elected officials, and many saw it specifically as a disenfranchisement of people of color. The *New National Era*, a national weekly magazine for Negroes, agreed, labeling the plan a step backward. Yet Negroes continued to vote, although never occupying more than five of the twenty-two House of Delegates seats. President Grant appointed three Negroes to the Governor's Council and John Mercer Langston, an Ohio-born Negro who had come to Washington to head Howard University's law school, as legal counsel to the Board of Health. At the same time James Wormley and his son William, former mayor Bowen, and Maj. Gen. Oliver O. Howard, president of Howard University, signed a petition recommending John Langston as trustee for the colored schools.[1]

White appointees included Henry Cooke, Grant's intimate and the brother and partner of one of Grant's staunchest financial supporters, Jay Cooke, to the governorship and president ex-officio of the Board of Public Works, and Alexander Shepherd, another member of Grant's inner circle, as vice president of the board. Owing to his take-charge confidence and engaging personality, Shepherd had Governor Cooke and other territorial officials deferring to him from the start. As the *Daily Patriot* wryly commented, "Why is the Governor like a gentle lamb? Because he is led by A. Shepherd."[2]

Years before his appointment to the Board of Public Works, Shepherd's consuming passion had been to make the backwater that served as the capital into a city worthy of the country's growing power. During the war the streets had been paved, but not enough to prevent rain from turning thoroughfares into bogs of mud. Deserted forts were decaying, and an antiquated sewerage system endangered residents' health. Shepherd wanted to transform this shabby, sprawling unfinished town into a modern metropolis. His objective strongly appealed to President Grant, who gave his blessing to Shepherd's full-speed-ahead style. Only three weeks after his induction as vice president of the board, Shepherd produced his comprehensive plan. The original design of Maj. Pierre L'Enfant, the famous French engineer George Washington had hired to map out the new federal city, which Shepherd lamented had for decades lain unfulfilled, was to be realized. To do so, Shepherd began with drainage, grading, and paving. Tiber Creek became the principal sewer of the district, draining water from northwest Washington and Georgetown into the Potomac. Uniform grades on the principal thoroughfares and avenues were set in place in order to execute L'Enfant's majestic vistas. Streets and sidewalks were paved with wood, asphalt, stone, or macadam.

Understanding that he had his best shot at achieving his dream under this administration, Shepherd moved fast. In a little more than two years he brought forth 58.5 miles of wooden pavement, 28.5 miles of concrete, and 93 miles of cobble, macadam, gravel, and Belgian block, 208 miles of sidewalk, 123 miles of sewers, 3,000 gas lamps; and 60,000 planted trees.[3] Free of local control, he had literally transformed Washington overnight, making it the best-lit and best-paved city in the country.

In pulling off his miracle, Shepherd provided nearly full employment for colored and white laborers, and even when New York and Philadelphia firms landed Public Works contracts and brought their own workers, Washingtonians got work. But to get more money than Congress had originally allotted, Shepherd coerced his workers to vote for large public bond issues and raised assessments on local property. As a result, many homeowners, including Negroes, were forced to foreclose. By September 1872 sixteen eight-column pages of fine print in the *Evening Star* listed properties that were to be sold at auction for nonpayment of taxes.[4] Making matters worse for Negroes, the Freedmen's Bureau ended activity in 1872, leaving the needy colored population with no federal agency to turn to for help. Set up in 1865 at the close of the Civil War to help the hundreds of thousands of penniless Negroes by supplying necessities and setting up supervised contracts between freedmen and their employers to protect Negroes' rights, the creation of the bureau embodied the widespread belief among Republicans that the federal government must take some responsibility for the emancipated slaves. After spending $17 million, the bureau closed down.

One bureau still helped the poor, albeit in an indirect way, and that was the Bureau of Public Health. Its employees conducted sanitary inspections in every home. In slum areas the board insisted that landlords provide tenants with adequate facilities. The board doubled the number of garbage and rubbish collections each week and hired the Odorless Excavating Apparatus Company to remove night soil from privies by suction pumps and empty it into airtight containers. Health officials condemned the worst tenements and demolished several hundred irreparably unsanitary dwellings. As a result of this activity, Langston, as counsel of the board and its most visible figure, became admired in both white and Negro Washington.

Because of widespread complaints from all economic and racial segments of Washington society, the House of Representatives felt compelled to respond, which it did by conducting an investigation into the finances of the Board of Public Works. Not surprisingly, the House vindicated Shepherd of any wrongdoing, although it mildly reprimanded him for extravagance, for the simple reason that his renovations greatly benefited the federal government and the city. Before Shepherd's Public Works few residents, including congressmen, ventured out at night. Not only did the new broad, smoothly paved, and well-illuminated avenues stimulate a lively nightlife, these vast improvements attracted industrialists from New York, New England, and Pennsylvania, and men who had made fortunes in gold and silver mines in the West.

By late 1872 and early 1873 the nation's production was almost twice its 1865 level, a figure all the more impressive in view of the South's stagnation and the three million immigrants who came to the North and West seeking jobs. The

United States, having become in these short eight years second only to England in manufacturing production, had irrevocably entered the industrial age. During these same eight years 35,000 miles of railroad track were laid. The railroad reduced transportation costs, established a national market, and helped speed the country toward becoming the preeminent industrial nation. Along the way hundreds of millionaires emerged, many of whom went to Washington to effect favorable regulations and subsidies for their businesses. Mark Twain, who spent a winter in Washington as secretary to a senator, satirized these "parvenus," so different from the Southerners of antebellum Washington, in *The Gilded Age*. Their conspicuous consumption and neverending balls, receptions, buffets, and picnics contrasted starkly with the lives led by the majority of Washington dwellers.

While the rich entertained and laborers sought higher wages, the bank Jay Cooke and Company, which Gov. Henry Cooke represented in the capital, neared collapse. Jay Cooke had been unable to sell bonds in a market already glutted with railroad securities for the Northern Pacific Railroad that he was building from Duluth, Minnesota, to Tacoma, Washington. As a result he'd had to put more and more of his company's banking capital into the railroad. At the same time he worried that the House's exoneration of the Board of Public Works' financing practices was a whitewash, so he urged his brother to resign as governor. Henry Cooke got out on September 13, 1873. Grant nominated Shepherd to succeed Cooke; he was promptly confirmed by the Senate. On September 16 Shepherd was inaugurated as governor of the Public Works Board at Henry Cooke's Georgetown mansion. The following evening President Grant visited Jay Cooke at Ogontz, his 380-acre estate north of Philadelphia. A fifty-two-room gilded showplace, Ogontz cost Cooke a million dollars. During breakfast with Grant the next morning, Cooke received a telegram informing him that his New York partner, refusing any further Northern Pacific Railroad subsidy, closed the doors of the Manhattan office of Jay Cooke and Company. Cooke said nothing, but when the president and his party left, he gave orders to close the Philadelphia and Washington branches. Within days a financial panic engulfed the nation's credit system. Banks and brokerage companies went bust, the stock market suspended operation, and factories laid off workers, setting off a depression that lasted for five long years.

In Washington, schoolteachers, clerks in the District government offices, police, firemen, and street department workers went unpaid. Every public service deteriorated. Cuts in the Board of Health reduced its efficiency; want increased petty crime; schools could accommodate less than half of the District's colored children. The *New National Era* ceased publication due to financial difficulties, depriving the public of the best gauge of Negro opinion and Negroes of their only paper of protest against injustice. The city of Washington declared bankruptcy.

By the summer of 1874 Congress pronounced the territorial government a failure, voted to abolish the governorship, the legislature, and the Board of Public Works, singling out Alexander Shepherd as the perpetrator of sloppy, extravagant management—he had gone $10 million over the $10 million budgeted for improvements—and put control of the District in the hands of three commissioners to be appointed by the president. The U.S. government stood behind fifty-year bonds to pay the $20 million deficit. All elective offices disappeared, and along with them Negro suffrage. The *Georgetown Courier* praised this development for disposing of the "curse" of the Negro vote.[5]

Henry Cooke disappeared from sight, and Alexander Shepherd and his family moved to Mexico. Negroes were cut off from contact with whites, which local politics had created. Howard University managed to stay open only by dropping courses and halving faculty salaries. The Freedman's Bank failed, wiping out the savings of hundreds of Negro families. Unemployment rose to new peaks. The Navy Yard fired four hundred employees and the Bureau of Engraving seven hundred. The newly appointed commissioners drastically reduced the number of people on the District payroll and cut common laborers' wages from a dollar fifty to a dollar a day. Although black representation in Congress reached a Reconstruction peak of eight in 1875, life for Negroes worsened in the city. The depression deepened so that by 1876 Rep. Adlai Stevenson of Illinois begged the House to appropriate $20,000 to lessen the "absolute starvation in the city."[6]

In contrast to the plight of so many, James Wormley continued to prosper. Even though Wormley's was the city's most expensive hotel, it nearly always commanded full occupancy. Europeans especially appreciated Wormley's attention to detail and concern for their comfort, qualities they found missing in other American hotels. Dutch travelers quite naturally leaned toward Wormley's since their entire Foreign Service delegation resided there. So many English writers had stayed at Wormley's and written favorably about the experience that their countrymen most often chose to stay there. John Hay, who had entered the Foreign Service as secretary to U.S. legations in Paris, Vienna, and Madrid after Lincoln's assassination, had lived at Wormley's for a time after returning to this country and recommended the hotel to his many French, Austrian, and Spanish friends. The German delegation, representing the newly united Germany, lived at the hotel during most of the 1870s.

Prominent Americans came as well. Writer and brother of James T.'s Civil War commander, Henry Adams; his wife, Clover; and their good friend, the noted geologist Clarence King, stayed there. Wormley asked King to examine and estimate the worth of nuggets of gold he had brought back to Washington from his gold prospecting days. Government officials put on big dinners and gave receptions there on a regular basis. And many congressmen, among them Rep. Benjamin Eames of Rhode Island, Sen. Roscoe Conkling of New York, Rep. Frank Hurd of Ohio, Sen. Lot Morrill of Vermont, and representatives William Crapo and Henry Pierce of Massachusetts lived, at one time or another, at the hotel. When alive, Charles Sumner was often seen at the hotel, as Wormley attended to many housekeeping matters at Sumner's home, and the two men often talked about pending civil rights legislation. After the Massachusetts senator died, Wormley bought much of his furniture to furnish what came to be called the Sumner parlor. Then he hired the "Painter of Presidents" Henry Ulke to do Sumner's portrait and one of Sen. Samuel Hooper, Clover Adams's uncle and hotel mortgagor until he died in 1875, to hang in the parlor. Other local artists, Peter Baumgrass in particular, did commissioned portraits of other prominent Washingtonians, which lined the walls of other common rooms in the hotel. So often did natives of Massachusetts frequent the hotel, whether as residents, overnight guests, or restaurant patrons, it seemed only appropriate that when former Massachusetts senator and vice president Henry Wilson died at the end of November 1875, James Wormley was asked to be part of the honor guard that accompanied his remains to Boston for burial.

Besides the hotel, James Wormley continued to operate his I Street businesses, including the rooming house at 1527 I Street, NW.[7] Used to accommodate overflow guests, it was referred to as the Branch Hotel. To supply fresh vegetables and meat for the hotel, he and his oldest son, William, bought land along the northeast line of Pierce Mill Road, northwest of where Van Ness Street now crosses Reno Road in an area called Tenleytown. As the highest point of elevation in the city at 420 feet above sea level, Tenleytown was the site of Fort Reno, the largest Civil War stronghold in the city. A lot like a small, sleepy village, Tenleytown had always been incorporated as part of the District of Columbia, although for Washingtonians it was "country."[8]

The Wormley property included three large houses and a frame building. Sons William and Garrett occupied two of the houses with their wives and children and servants, and James and Anna lived in the third. Each house had eleven good-sized rooms plus pantry, bathrooms, hot and cold water supply, and stables. As luxurious as the houses were, what the family loved above all else were the groves of huge beech and oak trees.[9]

The frame building became an upscale roadhouse frequented by Washington celebrities and owners of race horses.[10] With its commodious stables and a race track, the property became a popular place for owners to train their horses. Yet another extension of the hotel, the house became known as Wormley's Clubhouse, a favorite breakfast and dinner rendezvous.

Wormley frequently entertained special hotel guests at his home or at the roadhouse. His habit was to send one of the hotel's carriages to fetch his visitors and after dinner take them back to the central city. Francis J. Grimké, pastor of the Fifteenth Street Colored Presbyterian Church, described one of these evenings in a letter to Wormley's grandson, G. Smith Wormley:

> I remember spending one evening with him in company with Dr. Edward Wilmot Blyden, the noted African scholar, at his farm, a little out of the city. We were both invited by him, and were driven out in one of his vehicles. It was a very pleasant evening. We talked about many things, especially bearing on the race question. And among them, of the Commission which President Grant had sent to Haiti and on which Mr. Douglass had a place. There was something about the affair that greatly displeased Mr. Wormley. I cannot now recall exactly what it was; but I do remember very distinctly that he was much wrought up over it, and expressed himself in very forceful language.[11]

Grimké is describing a dinner that took place well over a half-century earlier, so he can be forgiven for having confused the Dominican Republic with Haiti, since the two countries make up the island of Hispaniola. Moreover, Frederick Douglass did have a Haiti connection, having been appointed consul general of Haiti in 1889, five years after Wormley's death. Wormley was referring to Douglass's appointment as assistant secretary to the commission that President Grant sent to the Dominican Republic in 1871.

There are a number of reasons why Wormley should have been wrought up, and he said so far more forcibly than Grimké was willing to divulge to his grandson. Grimké did, however, tell a contemporary that Wormley felt Douglass had compromised his dignity in accepting Grant's commission:

> He regarded the offer as an insult; and in expressing himself in regard to it

used very strong language. He said, if he had been in Mr. Douglass' place, and it had been offered to him, he would have spit in General Grant's face and he meant it. He seemed greatly wrought up. From what I could gather from the tenor of Mr. Wormley's remarks, Mr. Douglass was named as Secretary of the Commission, but was not *expected* to act; some white man was to be the real secretary, Mr. Douglass' name being used merely to get his influence, hoping thereby to aid in the accomplishment of General Grant's purpose.[12]

In his remarks to his friend, Grimké is closer to the mark. President Grant wanted to annex the Dominican Republic to establish an all-black American state to which former slaves would emigrate. He sent his secretary, Orville Babcock, at the time living in the White House, with two Texans to negotiate to buy the Dominican Republic. The treaty they drew up was referred to as the Santo Domingo treaty, after the Dominican Republic's largest city. Charles Sumner, at the time chairman of the Foreign Relations Committee, opposed the treaty. He was disgusted that instead of solving the racial problems within the continental United States, the president espoused a latter-day colonizationist scheme. "Nor can it be forgotten," Sumner said in a letter to two dozen Washington Negroes, including James's son William, "that shortly afterward, on the return of the commission from this island, Hon. Frederick Douglass, the colored orator, accomplished in manners as in eloquence, was thrust away from the company of the Commissioners at the common table of the mail-packet on the Potomac, almost within sight of the Executive Mansion, simply on account of his color; but the President, at whose invitation he had joined the Commission, never uttered a word in condemnation of this exclusion, and when entertaining the returned Commissioners at [a White House] dinner carefully omitted Mr. Douglass, who was in Washington at the time, and thus repeated the indignity."[13] Sumner had been outraged by the willingness of Douglass to lend his name to the annexation, and he spoke of this often with James Wormley. After the treaty died in the Senate, Grant saw to it that Sumner lost his chairmanship of foreign affairs.

Grimké told Wormley's grandson that their evening with Dr. Blyden ended with "a delicious oyster supper." He also praised Wormley for not shutting "the door of his hotel against a member of his own race" because, he said, Wormley "was a race man, in the sense that he was thoroughly interested in the welfare of his race."[14] Grimké could have added, even if Wormley's concern for his race cost him money.

In the fall of 1875, Chicago lawyer Emory Storrs, who had been hired to represent Orville Babcock in the Whiskey Ring Affair, went to Washington to do interviews and research. He took a suite at Wormley's for himself, his wife, and his son. When Storrs checked out of the hotel, "where he dispensed a princely hospitality," he paid his $1,500 bill with a check.[15] The check bounced and Wormley never got his money. Months after Babcock's acquittal in early 1876, Storrs started campaigning for Republicans. Having learned about Storrs's unpaid bill, a Democratic congressional committeeman went to Wormley to ask if the hotelier still had the dishonored check. In his safe, Wormley said. "I will give you the face value of the check for it, Mr. Wormley." Why, Wormley asked. Told that Storrs was hurting Democrats and that he planned to use the check to embarrass Storrs, Wormley replied, "The check is not for sale. I am a Republican and my race owes its freedom and its opportunities to the Republican Party."[16]

His race owed a lot to men like himself as well. Wormley had benefited from the strong sense of solidarity within the District's Negro community, and he intended to do nothing to undermine it. Before Emancipation, free people of color had provided assistance to slaves, frequently collecting money to buy out slaves in difficulty with their masters. James Wormley's good friend, minister and educator John F. Cook, to cite one example, gained his freedom from the hard work of an aunt. Several of the District's slaveholders allowed slaves to work during their free time to earn money to buy their freedom. Such a slave was Cook's aunt Alethia Tanner, who operated a vegetable garden near the White House during her free time.[17] With the money she earned—President Jefferson had been one of her customers—she purchased her own freedom in 1810. In 1826 she bought her older sister and five of her children, one of whom was Cook. In all, Alethia Tanner helped to free eighteen slaves. To cite another example, Anna Thompson Wormley, James's wife, purchased the freedom of Samuel Jones of Hagerstown, Maryland, which he repaid by working for a time in her husband's livery business.[18] After the Civil War the community formed fraternal, benevolent, and mutual aid societies, some to bury the dead, some to put out fires, and others to educate children and themselves. These mutual aid societies extended help to destitute nonmembers as well. Scattered all over Washington, the Negro community had developed a cohesiveness that began in their churches.

In the 1820s and 1830s, when Negroes first began attending churches in significant numbers, Washington's Protestant churches segregated the colored by restricting them to the balconies and not allowing them to participate in the churches' social affairs or to hold church offices. In one church colored members left because the minister was a slaveholder; in another the white minister refused to hold colored babies in his arms for baptism; and in still another, colored members had to enter by an outside gallery. As early as 1820, when colored members of the Ebenezer Church broke away and founded the Israel Metropolitan Christian M.E. Church, until after the Civil War, Negroes formed their own churches.[19] In 1841 they formed their own Presbyterian church at Fifteenth and H Streets. John F. Cook and later Francis Grimké, both close to the entire Wormley clan, had been pastors. Then the Methodists separated; next the Baptists. James Wormley's youngest child and only daughter, Anna, and his oldest child, William, and a daughter-in-law (Garrett's wife, the sister of Henry Adams's coachman) were cofounders of the Berean Baptist Church. Twenty-two members of the Nineteenth Street Baptist Church met at William's residence at 1126 Sixteenth Street, NW, to form this new congregation. When a council of Baptist churches recognized the new group in June of 1877, it got a pastor who volunteered his services and then built a church on Eighteenth Street. They grew from twenty-two to two hundred members. Anna donated the church's organ.[20] The Unitarian Church, which sprang from New England roots, maintained a colored membership and actually became a "hotbed" of abolitionism. The Catholic Church had from the first practiced nondiscriminatory religion. It had been its worldwide tradition to support integrated services and schools. A product of this integration, Patrick Healy, became a professor at Georgetown University, then acting president in 1873, and president in 1874.

Even though Catholic churches had been fully integrated, many colored parishioners of St. Matthews, a Catholic church across the street from Wormley's Hotel, began construction of their own parish, St. Augustine's, at the same time Father Healy became president of Georgetown. To reduce costs, the men of the parish dug the foundation, working every evening after their customary jobs. Finished in 1876, the church's interior included a hand-carved pulpit designed by the church's architect to harmonize with its Gothic exterior. James Wormley donated the pulpit.[21]

Wormley apparently had been generous in many directions, as his extant papers show. Thank-you letters reveal he donated food to the city's orphan asylums, gave gifts to multiple charities, forgave loans, and loaned money freely. But Wormley helped his race in other than monetary ways. When his son William was appointed a trustee of the colored public schools for Washington and Georgetown in 1870, his father publicly supported integrating the public schools.

The first public school system in the District was established at the end of 1804, but it was for white children only. Although no provisions had been made for the public education of colored children, even though Negroes paid taxes, a group of former slaves founded the first school for colored students on Capitol Hill in 1807. Since the founders were illiterate, they engaged a white teacher to instruct the students. This led to the founding of fifty-two other colored day schools, twelve sponsored by whites and forty by blacks, until finally, in 1864, an act establishing public schools for colored children was passed—though not until 1866 could enough money be found to open the first public school for these children.[22] The next step was an integrated school system; accordingly, a District school integration bill became an annual fixture on the congressional agenda. In the Senate on February 8, 1871, Charles Sumner opposed a motion by Senator Patterson of New Hampshire, chairman of the Committee for the District, to strike out a clause from a pending District school bill that would end existing segregated schools. In making his argument he read a statement that had been prepared by James Wormley. Late in 1873 a committee of prominent men that included James Wormley called on Gov. Henry Cooke to push integration of the public school system. Despite Wormley's and others' efforts, no action was taken. Even so, this period was the Golden Age for Washington's people of color.

With a black president of Georgetown University, public schools for Negroes that Congress had decreed must be supported on a pro rata basis, two centers of higher learning—Howard University and Wayland Seminary—under way, blacks as messengers, clerks, and a few as officials in the federal and municipal bureaucracies, a black man, James Wormley, owning the city's most luxurious hotel, with Frederick Douglass (newly settled in the District) and the Reverend Martin Sella putting out a respected weekly newspaper—with all this, the future for blacks in Washington seemed assured. Not surprising, then, that in late 1873, the *New National Era* concluded that "probably to a greater extent than elsewhere in the country is the equality in the matter of public rights accorded in the District of Columbia. . . . Our only drawback today is in the matter of schools."[23] In fact, the great drawback at the time was the Supreme Court, which in three decisions emasculated the postwar Fourteenth and Fifteenth Amendments, a devastating development since Congress had placed the burden of enforcing the freedmen's civil rights on the federal judiciary.

The first civil rights law in U.S. history, the Civil Rights Act of 1866, gave jurisdiction to federal courts for "all causes, civil and criminal, affecting persons who are denied or cannot enforce in the courts or judicial tribunals of the state, locality, where they may be, any of the rights secured to them" for reasons of race.[24] In the same year the Fourteenth Amendment passed, significant because it was the Constitution's first commitment to equality. Of the amendment's five sections, the first and fifth became pivotal in the litigation for Negro rights.

The first section says: "All persons born or naturalized in the United States, and subject to the jurisdiction thereof, are citizens of the United States and of the state wherein they reside. No State shall make or enforce any law which shall abridge the privileges or immunities of citizens of the United States; nor shall any State deprive any person of life, liberty, or property, without due process of law; nor deny to any person within its jurisdiction the equal protection of laws." This section emphasizes that national citizenship is primary and state citizenship derivative from it; as a result, the state is prohibited from passing any law that would compromise the protections guaranteed to citizens by the Constitution. Section 5 says, "The Congress shall have power to enforce, by appropriate legislation, the provisions of this article." In other words, Congress gave itself the authority to pass laws in order to execute terms of the amendment.

A year later, on February 26, 1869, Congress passed the Fifteenth Amendment that said, "The right of citizens of the United States to vote shall not be denied or abridged . . . on account of race, color, or previous condition of servitude."

Southern Democrats invoked states' rights principles to fight the legislation. In Pulaski, Tennessee, in June of 1866, six Confederate veterans met in the law office of Thomas M. Jones to start the Ku Klux Klan, a citizens' organization whose purpose was to impede the implementation of the Civil Rights Act. Within a year the group reorganized as the Invisible Empire of the South with a grand wizard as its head. Klansmen spread all over the South, threatening Negroes and their white allies. Before long, similar groups sprang up. To retaliate Congress passed the Enforcement Act of 1870 to facilitate federal prosecution of private individuals who committed criminal acts based on race in cases where state officials failed to act. Within a year Congress moved to strengthen the Enforcement Act with the Ku Klux Klan Act of 1871.

This amazing body of law, the Thirteenth, Fourteenth, and Fifteenth Amendments together with the civil rights and enforcement legislation, created a new Constitution that extended to Negroes full rights of citizenship, established for the first time in U.S. history a constitutional guarantee of equality, and empowered the federal government to protect the fundamental rights of its citizens.

These laws gave Washington power over matters that had since the beginning of the Republic been the sole jurisdiction of the states. These laws worked fairly well for three or four years, even though implementation was difficult. Shortages of troops, money, courts, and an abundance of Southern intransigence meant that it was only a matter of time until a case testing the reach and meaning of these new laws would reach the Supreme Court.

The first test came in 1873 in the Slaughterhouse Cases, and, oddly enough, the rights of Negroes were not involved. In 1869 the state of Louisiana had sought to regulate the slaughtering of livestock in Orleans (New Orleans), Jefferson, and St. Bernard Parishes (in Louisiana, a parish is the equivalent of a county) by granting a monopoly to one company. The justification was health. Every business day stock dealers landed hundreds of cattle, pigs, and sheep at Slaughterhouse Point, a few miles from New Orleans, and drove the terrified animals through the streets to various slaughterhouses where butchers killed, skinned, gutted, and hung their carcasses on hooks to dangle unrefrigerated for hours and sometimes days. The butchers then threw the gory waste into the streets or river, further poisoning the city's air and water. New Orleans was a city with no public sewer system, infamously filthy and disease-ridden. No matter how unsanitary their practice proved to be, butchers in the area claimed that the statute violated the Fourteenth Amendment by depriving them of their citizenship right to property, in this case to make a living, one of those privileges and immunities guaranteed to citizens of the United States. The vote was five to four against the application of the amendment to the Slaughterhouse Cases. Justice Samuel F. Miller rejected the butchers' plea, insisting that Congress had intended primarily to give citizenship rights to former slaves. Had he stopped there, the decision would not have been onerous. But he went on to say that the amendment protected only federal rights, like access to ports and navigable waterways, the right to run for federal office, travel to the seat of government, and be protected on the high seas. Not many freedmen cared much about these rights. Finally, Miller said, the Fourteenth Amendment had not fundamentally altered traditional federalism in the sense that most citizens' rights remained under state control, and with these the amendment had "nothing to do."[25] By holding that there were still two categories of citizens—national and state—and that the privileges-and-immunities clause did not protect rights flowing from state citizenship but only those arising out of national citizenship, the majority of the court substantially repudiated the Fourteenth Amendment. Dissenting, Justice Stephen J. Field said that if this were the amendment's meaning, "It was a vain and idle enactment, which accomplished nothing and most unnecessarily excited Congress and the people on its passage."[26] Field's dissent certainly seems more in keeping with Congress's intent in drafting the amendment, which clearly bans states from limiting the "privileges and immunities" of U.S. citizens. The Fourteenth Amendment furthermore specifically orders states to respect all citizens' rights to "due process" and "equal protection under the laws." Another of the Court's minority of four, Justice Noah H. Swayne, angrily declared, "This Court has no authority to interpolate a limitation that is neither express nor implied. Our duty is to execute the law, not to make it."[27]

The second decision, *United States v. Cruikshank*, came in 1876. The case arose from the Colfax Massacre, the bloodiest act of terrorism during Reconstruction. The 1872 gubernatorial election in Louisiana, characterized by fraud and intimidation, produced two rival claimants for the governorship, Democrat John McEnery and Republican William Kellogg, causing unrest all over the state. In the tiny village of Colfax in Grant Parish, a Democrat and a Republican each claimed to have won the office of sheriff. The Grant administration recognized William Kellogg as the rightful governor. Kellogg sent rifles to the Republican claimant for sheriff in order to arm his almost entirely black followers. The Democratic claimant and his supporters, all white, launched an attack on the black Republicans when they were meeting in the courthouse. When the blacks inside refused to vacate, a torch was put to the building. Some of the occupiers died in the flames while others were shot as they fled the burning building. The twenty who had been taken prisoners were taken out of the jail the night after the battle and shot in cold blood. Figures vary as to how many Negroes were killed, ranging from a low of 60 to a high of 250. Seventy-seven years later, in 1950, the Louisiana Department of Commerce and Industry erected a plaque that reads, "On this site occurred the Colfax Riot in which three white men and 150 Negroes were slain. This event on April 13, 1873 marked the end of carpetbag misrule in the South." A more accurate caption that reflects how most white Southerners viewed the massacre at the time appears on a marble obelisk, a dozen feet high, in the Colfax white cemetery: "In loving remembrance erected to the memory of the [three] heroes who fell in the Colfax Riot fighting for white supremacy. April 13, 1873."

The nine white men accused of having taken part in the killing were arrested and put on trial in federal court in New Orleans, 220 miles southeast of Colfax. They were charged with having deprived the murdered men of their civil rights in contravention of the Enforcement Acts. After a mistrial, in a second trial four of the accused, including a William B. Cruikshank, were convicted. The conviction was appealed and heard by the U.S. Circuit Court of Appeals, which for this case consisted of the trial judge and of Associate Justice Joseph P. Bradley of the Supreme Court. Under the practice of the time, each Supreme Court justice was assigned a circuit to which he repaired for two or three months each year, sitting as a jurist and hearing appeals. The Supreme Court term in 1874 had ended May 4, whereupon Bradley left Washington for New Orleans. The trial judge voted to uphold the conviction, but Justice Bradley concluded that the power of Congress to enforce the two Reconstruction amendments did not include the power to provide punishment if the crime was punishable under the law of the state where it took place, the same reasoning he had used in the Slaughterhouse Cases. Since the Circuit Court judges disagreed, the matter went to the Supreme Court. Finally on March 27, 1876, almost three years after the massacre, the convictions of William Cruikshank and his companions were reversed. The majority opinion, in effect agreeing with Bradley's earlier decision, was issued by the new chief justice Morrison Waite, who began with a general statement of principles, citing Slaughterhouse Cases: "The same person may be at the same time a citizen of the United States and a citizen of a State."[28] Then he went on to say that the Fourteenth Amendment gave Congress the power to prohibit state denial of life, liberty, or property without due process of law, but the Colfax murders had been the work of private parties, not the state of Louisiana. The implication was that this case should have been left for adjudication within the court system of Louisiana.

The decision in the Cruikshank case left the federal government almost powerless to protect freedmen except by the use of troops, and these ordinarily had to be requested by the legislature or the governor of the state. In fact, James R. Beckwith, U.S. attorney for the district of the Circuit Court of Louisiana and the man who had drawn the initial indictment in the Cruikshank case, wrote his boss, the attorney general, that after the circuit court's decision in the Cruikshank matter, "the armed White League organizations in the South from which the most grave and serious danger and consequences may be apprehended sprung into life or received their vitality from the action of Justice Bradley in the case."[29] The Enforcement Act and its proposed application in the Cruikshank case posed a classic instance for which the Fourteenth Amendment and enforcing legislation were devised: the states had defaulted in their duty to protect citizens, so the federal government had to step in.

The Court decided in another case, the *United States v. Reese*, during the same term that it decided the Cruikshank case, and in the same narrow spirit. On January 30, 1873, William Garner, "of African descent," tried to vote in Lexington, Kentucky, in the city council election. Although he had satisfied all residency requirements, and although he had secured an affidavit showing that he had tried to pay the requisite $1.50 poll tax but had been wrongfully turned away on account of his race, Hiram Reese, an election inspector, refused to let him vote. Reese was indicted in federal court in Louisville for violating the third and fourth sections of the 1870 Enforcement Act, which prohibited interference with the right to vote. The case was argued before two judges who differed, causing Reese to go to the Supreme Court in 1875. The majority decision, handed down on March 27, 1876, once again upheld the primacy of state powers. Speaking for the majority, Chief Justice Waite held unconstitutional two significant provisions of the Enforcement Act of 1870, namely sections 3 and 4, which posited punishment for the wrongful acts of election officials against "citizens." Since a white official could be indicted for wrongful acts against a potential white voter under a literal reading of the law, Congress had intruded itself into an area for which it had no constitutional authorization given the objectives and limits of the Fifteenth Amendment. The indictments, then, must be dismissed because the statutes that had yielded them were unconstitutional. And then in what would become the most-quoted sentence Waite said that the Fifteenth Amendment does not confer the right of suffrage upon anyone.[30] Thus, he explained, although the amendment did give citizens a new constitutional right, that right was not the right to vote. That right, he continued, was exemption from discrimination in the exercise of the elective franchise on account of race, color, or previous condition of servitude. Prior to the Fifteenth Amendment, states could and did exclude citizens from voting based on age, property, education, or race. Now they could not use race. Associate Justice Nathan Clifford concurred in Waite's opinion, adding that even though Garner had twice tried to pay the poll tax, he did not have the means to pay it. Clifford used this unlikely assumption—unlikely because if someone did not have the $1.50, why would he offer to pay the amount not once but twice—to disqualify Garner, who had not fulfilled Kentucky's prerequisites for voting. Hiram Reese was cleared of any wrongdoing. Justice Ward Hunt issued the sole dissent, condemning the court's linguistic subtleties, "distinctions almost ridiculous." The dissent complained that this interpretation was as narrow as one could imagine. Because sections 1 and 2 specifically refer to "race" discrimination, obviously "citizens" in

3 and 4 meant persons of African descent, and just as obviously, the majority's interpretation was opposite to the known intent of Congress. Nevertheless, the majority held that regulations of elections remained primarily a state responsibility.

The impact of Slaughterhouse, Cruikshank, and Reese was devastating. In practical terms the Court had all but destroyed the legal basis for an effective federal presence in the South and gave white supremacists carte blanche to handle affairs as they saw fit. Illustrating the palpable effect of these decisions is the speed with which Enforcement Act cases in the South disappeared. In 1873 there had been more than twelve hundred cases brought; in 1874 almost a thousand; in 1875 just over two hundred.[31] By August 1876 the Augusta *Constitutionalist* noted publicly that since the enforcement laws had just recently been rendered nugatory by the Supreme Court, the much touted "bayonet program of the administration" was a mere scarecrow, "a scheme of bombast, full of sound and fury."[32] That a pamphlet put out by Southern Democrats that fall declared openly that the "administration has not troops enough to enforce its threats" indicates that most Southerners realized how impotent the federal government had become.

Because white supremacist groups like the Ku Klux Klan, Knights of the White Camellia, Knights of the Rising Sun, White Line, Constitutional Union Guards, Pale Faces, White Brotherhood, White League, Council of Safety, '76 Association, and who knows how many others, proliferated all over the South, intimidation and violence against Negroes increased. Yet these pro-states'-righters and anti-Reconstructionists had gotten a green light from the Supreme Court to move pretty much as they wished. As another presidential election approached, the survival of Reconstruction seemed hopeless. Even more ominous for the future, not only for the Negro in the South but for the survival of the nation as a whole, was the fact that by disarming those trying to maintain black access to the ballot, the Supreme Court decisions had brought on the most serious electoral crisis ever to confront the nation.

ELECTION

*I*n 1876 few in the nation realized as yet how little of Reconstruction endured. In eight states there was no longer even a pretense, for the states' righters had come to power and "redeemed" them—that is, reestablished self-government of the state. Only South Carolina, Louisiana, and Florida had not been "redeemed"; federal troops, albeit in pitifully small numbers and nearly impotent, survived. If Reconstruction on such shaky terms as these depended on a Republican presidency, then matters were indeed bleak. The party's capacity to hold on to the White House appeared to be at stake. Born in the summer of 1854 as an angry Northern reaction to the Kansas-Nebraska Act, the Republican Party had grown out of a single compelling issue. In order to enhance the economic feasibility of a transcontinental railroad from Illinois to California, Illinois Democrat senator Stephen Douglas introduced the Kansas-Nebraska Act to foster rapid settlement in the West. When Southern senators opposed the act, Douglas added a provision that repealed the Missouri Compromise line, and in so doing made slavery north of the line, specifically in Kansas and Nebraska, possible if the settlers wanted it. Yet the reason that opponents of slavery had supported the Missouri Compromise was that they saw containment as the first step to the extinction of an unmitigated moral evil. Within six and a half years this new Republican Party had elected a president. Then the ultimate expression of the states' rights dogma—secession—then civil war and Lincoln's assassination followed in rapid order. For the Republicans, the question of what to do about the defeated South became paramount. Because of the alarm raised by the thirteen new electoral votes gained by Democrats when the three-fifths clause in the Constitution disappeared as a result of emancipation; because of the uprising of Reform Republicans in 1872; because when Democrats captured the House of Representatives in 1874, they had done so by turning a Republican majority of 198 to 88 into a Democratic majority of 169 to 109; and because Democrats had also won nineteen of twenty-five governor races in 1874, there emerged in 1876 for the first time in the Republican Party's short history a real choice of nominees for president.

Reform, the overriding issue of the campaign, had arisen from the ceaseless revelations of wrongdoing that had emanated from Washington. A thousand Republican delegates and alternates, fifty Negroes among them, made their way to Cincinnati for the sixth nominating convention of their party. Their leading candidate was Maine representative James G. Blaine, Speaker of the House. When a newspaper broke the story that Blaine had used his influence as Speaker to secure a land grant for an Arkansas railroad in which he owned stock, and that Union Pacific, another government-subsidized railroad, had accepted this stock as collateral for a loan Blaine never repaid, Liberal Republicans decided to back Benjamin Bristow. Bristow had impeccable reform credentials as the prosecutor of the Whiskey Ring perpetrators when he was secretary of the treasury. The third major contender, Senator Roscoe Conkling of New York, was Grant's man, hardly an asset in what purported to be a reform election. The last of the candidates deemed to have a crack at the nomination, Senator Oliver Morton of Indiana, had solid executive and legislative accomplishments, but a paralytic stroke in 1865 had left him permanently, if partially, disabled. Three others—Postmaster General Marshall Jewell of Connecticut, Gov. John Hartkranft of Pennsylvania, and Gov. Rutherford Hayes of Ohio—were favorite sons.[1]

In 1876, Cincinnati was the nation's eighth largest city with 250,000 residents, most of whom made their living in pork packing or beer brewing, and they were proud that their city had been chosen twice to host a Republican gathering. In 1872 the Liberal Republicans had nominated Horace Greeley in the same twin-towered Exposition Hall, a gargantuan warehouse that looked like a railroad depot with the tracks removed, toward which delegates, alternates, ward bosses, newspaper reporters, telegraphers, souvenir and food vendors, and hangers-on made their way on Wednesday morning, June 14. As ticket holders moved into their assigned areas, the band played patriotic tunes. Opening speeches consumed the entire day.

The next day, hot and humid despite the city's location on the hills above the Ohio River, delegates suffered through nominating speeches and demonstrations.

Balloting started on Friday. A candidate needed 378 votes to become the party's nominee. On the first ballot Blaine led the pack with 285 votes. On the second he gained eleven votes while Conkling and Morton lost ground. Ballots three and four showed little change. By ballot five Blaine's solid lead began unraveling when Michigan cast its twenty-two votes for Rutherford B. Hayes. Blaine kept his lead at 286, but Hayes, who had hitherto trailed Blaine, Bristow, Conkling, and Morton, surged to third place. On the sixth ballot Blaine regained a command-ing lead with a total of 308 votes, but Hayes, with 113 votes, rose to second place. A stop-Blaine movement rallied to Hayes on the seventh ballot. On the eighth Indiana switched the bulk of its votes to Hayes. It then fell to New York to put one of the two leaders over the top. Although Senator Conkling had wanted the nomination, at this point in the balloting he knew he had no chance. He had de-tested Blaine ever since the Maine representative, ten years earlier in a debate on the floor of the House on an army bill of little import, referred to Conkling's "haughty disdain, his grandiloquent swell, his majestic, super-eminent turkey-gobbler strut." But was this insult enough motivation to cause Conkling to spurn the highly popular and oratorically gifted Speaker in order to anoint an unknown Midwestern governor? Apparently so, because sixty-one of New York's seventy votes went to Hayes and only nine to Blaine. This switch put Hayes over the top with 384 to Blaine's 351.

The convention finished its work by picking a vice presidential candidate. Party leaders concluded they should choose a New Yorker since Hayes's probable Democratic opponent, Tilden, was a New Yorker. They turned first to Chester Arthur, a Conkling lieutenant, but then backed off because as collector of cus-toms for the Port of New York—the choicest prize within the spoils system—he seemed an inappropriate choice as the second man to a candidate who promised to do away with this system. Instead they chose William Wheeler, an obscure New York member of the House whose excessive caution and obsessive concern with his physical well-being resembled Tilden's.

"Who is Wheeler?" Hayes asked his wife, at the same time the country was won-dering, who was Hayes?[2] "A third-rate non-entity, whose only recommendation is that he is obnoxious to no one," historian Henry Adams, himself the descendant of two presidents, answered in the *North American Review*. As if corroborating, Joseph Pulitzer, whose *New York World* had supported Bristow, wrote, "Hayes has never stolen. Good God, has it come to this?"[3] Even Hayes's supporters had but faint praise. Ohio senator John Sherman called Hayes "a good soldier, though not greatly distinguished as such . . . [in Congress] not a leading debater or manager in party tactics, but . . . sensible."[4] Edward Noyes, a shrewd Ohio politician and Hayes's convention manager, advised delegates to "give us a man of great purity of private life and an unexceptional public record."[5]

That was Rutherford B. Hayes. Nothing in the record of this "not greatly distinguished" man, as Senator John Sherman described him, compared to the public achievements of the famous and often spellbinding Blaine or the reforming zeal of Bristow, but these more eminent men had made enemies, and Hayes had not. In the end, that made all the difference.

Born in Delaware, Ohio, and educated at Kenyon College and Harvard Law School, Hayes entered Cincinnati politics as a Whig in 1851. In 1852 he married Lucy Webb with whom he sired eight children, three of whom died in childhood. He supported Lincoln, served as judge-advocate and as infantry brigade commander in the Civil War, rose to be a commissioned brigadier general and a brevetted major general of volunteers, and was elected to the House of Representatives from Ohio before he was out of uniform. He resigned from Congress to run for governor.

A lack of drama marked the Democratic convention that opened on June 27 in St. Louis, the first meeting of a major political party west of the Mississippi. The nation's fourth most populous city with half a million people, St. Louis stretched for six miles along the Mississippi River. Despite efforts of John Kelly, Boss Tweed's replacement as head of Tammany who tried to derail Tilden's plans, and despite the presence of five other candidates, all betting favored Tilden, who was nominated on the second ballot. Delegates then picked Gov. Thomas Hendricks of Indiana for the vice presidential spot.

The only news from this convention focused on the absence of a single Negro delegate, and on the growing power of the Southern Democrats. For the first time since the Civil War, Southerners had regained power in the party for the simple reason that they had "redeemed" eight of the eleven former Confederate states, and thus could assure the Democratic nominee a good number of electoral votes.

Hayes and Tilden had much in common. Both had been honest lawyers, Hayes with a run-of-the-mill practice and Tilden, the better known, with forty years of lucrative corporate practice. Both were financially well off, Hayes having inherited half a million dollars in real estate from an uncle and the wealthier Tilden having earned and wisely invested his millions. Both men had been state legislators and governors, Hayes for a longer period than Tilden. Both strongly supported the Union, Hayes in the army and Tilden, too old for military service, by calling for high taxation and issuance of war bonds to meet the costs of war, and by threatening to campaign against any Democrat who opposed Lincoln. Both candidates were college educated and both loved books. In Congress Hayes had served as chairman of the Library Committee, where he pushed passage in the House of the Senate's bill that shifted the Smithsonian's books to the Library of Congress, and more important, opened the library to all citizens. Tilden left his considerable fortune to the founding of a library that became the New York Public Library. Thus, each candidate had a powerful influence on the establishment of the nation's and perhaps the world's two greatest libraries. Both men favored civil service reform, and most relevant to this election, both favored the withdrawal of federal troops from the South.

According to custom, neither Tilden nor Hayes had been present at their conventions. After party leaders officially notified each of their nomination and after each issued a letter of acceptance, the campaign began. The appointment of Zachariah Chandler as the chairman of the Republican National Committee and as Chairman of the Hayes-Wheeler campaign stirred controversy, especially among reform Republicans. A big, affable political boss from Michigan, Zach Chandler had made a fortune in trade, banking, and land speculation and then got himself elected to the U.S. Senate in 1857, where he stayed until 1875. One of Grant's favorite cronies, he served as the secretary of the interior from 1875 to 1877. What made his appointment as Hayes's campaign manager absurd to many, in addition to the impropriety of a cabinet secretary running a presidential campaign, was his renown as the archenemy of civil service reform, the most important plank in the Republican platform and the principal goal of his candidate.

"Just think of a civil service reform party making Zach Chandler chairman," the *Nation* exploded.[6] "The campaign will be the most glaring satire on civil service reform imaginable," Carl Schurz wrote Hayes.[7] He must be made to decline, Schurz added. Chandler did not even like Hayes, associating him with the Liberal Republicans. He stayed on anyway and got to work. His first priority was money. He levied a 2 percent assessment on the salary of each federal employee, a practice that had been a standard feature of American politics for decades and one that Hayes had promised to end. Government employees knew not to deny Chandler. They remembered that in the fall of 1875, right after Grant had appointed him secretary of the interior, he fired the chief clerk of the patent office for having refused to pay an assessment. Although Hayes claimed to "hate assessments; they are all wrong," he said nothing publicly.[8]

Despite the involuntary "donation" from civil servants, Republicans still lacked sufficient funds for a national campaign. Chandler gave $5,000 as an example to other wealthy partisans to do likewise, but too many had been hurt in the Depression of 1873 that persisted into 1876. Desperate, the Republican National Committee resorted to outright threats. Shortly before the election, for example, the Treasury Department notified the National Bank Note Company that its lucrative contract with the government would not be renewed. The treasurer of National Bank Note conferred with the secretary of the treasury. When the cancellation was withdrawn, National Bank Note gave the Republican Party $10,000.[9]

Tilden unwisely decided to be his own campaign manager. Late in July 1876 he chose Abram S. Hewitt to be his managing front man. He could not have chosen anyone better. Hewitt inspired countless young people to get involved in the campaign. Don Dickinson, Democratic state chairman of Michigan, in a letter to Theodore Roosevelt, explained: "Hewitt was as true a patriot and as pure a man as ever lived, in my opinion. . . . Young men of force all over the country joined the Tilden standard, and went into the canvass of '76 with an energy and a *will* for success that of itself was so potent in winning votes."[10] Dickinson accurately confirmed what many others had said, namely that they were so impressed with Hewitt that since Hewitt followed Tilden, they, too, became Tilden men.

Abram Hewitt *was* an impressive man. He and his college friend, Edward Cooper, became partners in the iron business when Peter Cooper gave his son and his son's friend the Trenton Iron Works. Calling their newly formed firm Cooper and Hewitt, they became pioneers in making iron girders and beams. During the Civil War they produced gun barrel material for the U.S. government at production cost. After the war President Johnson appointed Hewitt a commissioner to the Paris Exhibition of 1867. What he learned there about iron and steel manufacturing resulted in his introduction of the open-hearth process for manufacturing steel in the United States. Hewitt knew Tilden as a neighbor in the Gramercy Park section of Manhattan, and it was this friendship that led to Hewitt's entering public life. Hewitt helped Tilden in the campaign against Tweed and then played a prominent part in the reorganization of Tammany Hall. In 1874 he entered Congress and in 1876 became chairman of the Democratic National Committee.

Whatever oddity Tilden found in the situation of his campaign manager's father-in-law also running for president in 1876, he never revealed. Abram Hewitt had married Sarah Cooper, his partner Edward's sister. The Greenback Party, which advocated governmental issuance of paper notes, nominated Sarah and Edward's father, eighty-five-year-old Peter Cooper, as their presidential candidate. Wealthy manufacturer and philanthropist, he was best known as the founder of Cooper Union, the first institution of its kind, offering free courses in the arts and sciences to both men and women. Hewitt, himself, became active in Cooper Union management and with his wife gave $600,000 to its endowment. Peter Cooper accepted his party's nomination as an opportunity to espouse publicly his strong view that it was time for Congress to take steps to halt the concentration of wealth in the hands of the buccaneering few, and to "legislate for the poor as well as the rich, who can take care of themselves."[11] Hewitt shared his father-in-law's view and practiced what he advocated. During the depression that had begun three years earlier, he and Edward Cooper kept as many men as possible employed, at great loss to themselves.

Like Chandler, Hewitt first had to raise money in order to be able to campaign, but unlike Chandler he could not depend on federal largesse. Even if he could have, it is unlikely he would have resorted to assessments, having tried to put a stop to the system in Congress. In fact a bill to this end passed in the House but was defeated in the Senate. At the start of the campaign Hewitt had $30,000 on hand. He asked Tilden for money, but the candidate preferred that contributions come from a large number of Democrats who could afford to contribute. Wealthy Democrats thought that a man as rich as Tilden should finance his own campaign. Hewitt and Edward Cooper dipped into their own funds and asked prominent Democrats to urge Tilden to donate. The candidate responded with a small amount. In the end the Democrats were forced to run a national campaign on a paltry $150,000.

Late in July the energetic Chandler set up national headquarters in the opulent Fifth Avenue Hotel in New York. He allotted considerable space to the National Committee of Union Veterans, whose charge was to organize Boys in Blues Clubs for Hayes in every city and town in the country that could muster at least a few Union veterans. Next he arranged for William Dean Howells, the dynamic editor of the *Atlantic Monthly*, to write a campaign biography, and then he assembled an army of orators to stump the country.

The two-pronged strategy of the Republican campaign was to vilify Tilden and to wave the bloody shirt.[12] Republicans called Tilden a cheat, claiming he had made a fraudulent income tax return for 1862. They used print and gossip to portray this timid, ascetic, secretive man as immoral, dishonest, and syphilitic, a drunkard, counterfeiter, and swindler. None of the charges was accurate, but because Tilden took so long to respond, some damage was undoubtedly done to his cause. By contrast, when Democrats accused Hayes of some wrongdoing, Hayes responded immediately, using newspapers to get his version out. When on September 30 the *Chicago Times*, to take one example, accused Hayes of pocketing $1,000 given for safekeeping by a soldier in his Civil War regiment who was then killed in the Battle of Winchester, right away Hayes put out facts and figures proving his innocence in the matter.

The country was growing somewhat weary of the bloody flag gambit, which the Republican Party had been waving since secession. On the floors of Congress Republicans said that Tilden had failed to contribute to the Union cause because, they claimed, he would rather see Union soldiers starve to death before he would give them a single penny. Blaine claimed that Tilden had said, "Every man in the U.S. Army that marched across southern soil was a trespasser and liable to suit for damages in an action of trespass."[13] Even Hayes, supposedly hidden away, took up the bloody shirt. He told Garfield, "Our main issue must be *It is not safe to allow the Rebellion to come into power.*"[14] And finally Republicans warned that a Democratic victory would result in federal payments of Confederate claims for wartime damages.

After setting up the campaign's road map, Chandler went to see Grant at his summer place in Long Branch. He persuaded the president to send additional troops to South Carolina, Louisiana, and Florida to protect Republican—that is, colored—voters.

As a member of the Banking and Currency Committee in the House, Abram Hewitt had to remain in Washington until the long session's end in August. Back in New York he set up the national Democratic headquarters in the Everett House, a far more modest establishment than the Fifth Avenue Hotel. Next, Hewitt prepared the most elaborate campaign textbook yet issued by any party, a volume of 750 pages detailing the administration's scandals with an overview of the results of congressional investigations, and expounding Tilden's views and record. Hewitt did the outline, hired the Washington correspondent of the *New York Sun*, A. M. Gibson, to help him, and wrote the arguments that went with the documentary material.

The staff of experts that Tilden had assembled for his nomination effort became the nucleus of the Literary Bureau, a printing house at 59 Liberty Street. Col.

William Pelton, Tilden's nephew, took charge of the bureau. Its writers turned out editorials, news releases, broadsides, and circulars for newspapers. They assembled a huge mailing list and sent out speeches. They enrolled Democrats in local clubs to ensure mass meetings for speakers and parades. They organized six hundred Uncle Sam Clubs in New York State and then set up Tilden Clubs, Hendricks Clubs, and Tilden and Hendricks Clubs all over the country. Henry Watterson, editor of the *Louisville Courier-Journal*, spent several weeks at headquarters helping with publicity and outlining methods of campaigning in the West and South. Other unofficial advisers included John Bigelow, probably Tilden's closest friend; Manton Marble, *New York World* journalist and part owner who wrote the Democratic Party's 1876 platform; and Richard Dana, Liberal Republican and wealthy Massachusetts lawyer who once ran for Congress against Ben Butler and lost by a walloping 91 percent of the vote.

Hewitt tried to apply Tilden's New York organizational methods in other parts of the country. In a sense there were thirty-eight campaigns for the presidency, one in each state of the union, but the scarcity of funds forced the national committee to concentrate on specific states—Indiana until October, then New York, New Jersey, and Connecticut. Little or nothing could be accomplished in Ohio, Pennsylvania, Wisconsin, South Carolina, or Louisiana. Often when funds were desperately needed, Hewitt had to refuse them. J. S. Boyd of Jacksonville, for example, came to national headquarters begging for campaign funds. "For ten thousand dollars I will *ensure* Florida for Tilden," he pleaded with Hewitt.[15] But the money Hewitt had on hand, money that Edward Cooper had collected, had been earmarked for the North. After payment for speakers, printers, postage, and rents, little was left for state committees.

Despite the lack of money, early returns on election night appeared to foretell a Democratic victory. Tilden carried New York, New Jersey, Connecticut, and Indiana, more than enough, together with expected victories in the far West and a solid South to make him then next president. Well before midnight it appeared to be over. Out in Columbus, Hayes sat out the returns with a small group of friends in the parlor of his home. Before Hayes went to bed he wrote in his diary that "the election resulted in the defeat of the Republicans after a very close contest."[16] In New York Zachariah Chandler came to the same conclusion and went to bed at eleven p.m.

As Hayes and Chandler slept, Gen. Daniel Sickles, known not so much for having lost a leg at Gettysburg as for having killed Philip Barton, the son of the man who wrote "The Star-Spangled Banner," because he was having an affair with Sickles's wife, stopped by Republican headquarters at midnight. Only the chief clerk, M. A. Clancy, was present, and he was busily packing up records and papers. Sickles sat at Chandler's desk and went over vote tallies. Suddenly it occurred to him that, although clearly Tilden had the popular vote, if South Carolina, Louisiana, and Florida, whose final vote counts had not been announced, went to Hayes, the Republicans could squeak to victory in the electoral college. Unilaterally he decided to send telegrams under Chandler's name to Republican officials in the three states. Clancy objected to the plan; then Chester Arthur appeared at headquarters. Sickles showed Arthur his figures and the telegrams he had drafted.

"General, if you advise it, I have no doubt the chief clerk will feel authorized to send off these telegrams with the signature of the chairman." "Certainly," Arthur replied. "Let them be sent off at once. It seems to me your forecast is accurate."[17] Arthur went home; Sickles ordered the packing to stop and waited until almost dawn, when he left the hotel.

In these same early hours of November 8, the editors of the staunchly Republican *New York Times* worried about what to say about the election for their early edition. As they looked for a way not to admit defeat, the chairman of the Democratic State Committee telegraphed at 3:45 a.m. asking for the paper's estimate of Tilden's electoral votes. That the Tilden people were unsure of the outcome emboldened them to call the election "In Doubt." Nearly every other paper in the nation called it a Democratic victory. Most, in fact, concurred with the *Chicago Daily News* that Tilden had won "by a very considerable majority of the electoral vote."[18]

John Reid, the managing editor of the *New York Times* who had been in Andersonville Prison during the war, was the strongest partisan of the group, so it was natural that when the editors "put the paper to bed," he walked over to the Fifth Avenue Hotel to confer with Zach Chandler. Once there he ran into W. E. Chandler, a national committeeman who had just arrived after voting in New Hampshire. Together they read copies of the telegrams on Zach Chandler's desk, went over the tallies once more, and decided that if Hayes took the three unredeemed states, he might win. They rushed to Zach Chandler's room and banged on the door until they awakened him. He knew nothing about the Sickles telegrams, but he gave them his blessing to do whatever they deemed best. Once again telegrams went to party heads in South Carolina, Louisiana, and Florida.

"Hayes is elected if we have carried South Carolina, Florida, and Louisiana. Can you hold your state? Answer at once."[19] The telegraph operator, believing that Hayes had lost, refused to charge the telegrams to the Republican National Committee. Reid told him to bill the *Times*.

When Zach Chandler arrived at his desk late on the morning of November 8, he learned that eight and a half million men had voted, more than in any previous presidential election, and that Tilden had a lead of a quarter of a million votes. Moreover, the Democrats with sixteen states were ahead with 184 electoral votes, but 185 were necessary for election.

The Republicans carried nineteen states but had only 166 electoral votes. Now he understood the urgency of John Reid and W. E. Chandler; if Hayes took all the nineteen electoral votes of the states in doubt—seven from South Carolina, eight from Louisiana, and four from Florida—he would be elected. Therefore, with no declared tally from these states, Chandler declared that Hayes had won. Using the private wire of Jay Gould, Chandler telegraphed the "news" to Grant in Philadelphia (Grant was the houseguest of George W. Childs, publisher of the *Public Ledger*) and urged him yet again to send still more troops south. As Henry Watterson wrote years later about the morning hours of November 8, "the story of this surprising discrepancy between midnight and daylight reads like a chapter of fiction."[20]

In the three unredeemed Southern states, Republicans had waged a desperate struggle for political survival. In South Carolina Democrats in Edgefield and Laurens Counties voted early and often and stopped Negroes from getting to the polls. This fraud enabled their party to claim a statewide victory of the legislature and the governorship while Republicans claimed the presidential race by 815 votes. In Louisiana returns gave majorities to Tilden of between 8,000 and 9,000.[21] As in South Carolina there was unquestionable fraud: overregistration of voters on the Republican side and "bulldozing," violence, and intimidation, especially in the five heavily Negro parishes of Morehouse, Ouachita, East Baton Rouge, East Feliciana, and West Feliciana on the Democratic side. The *New York Times* ran an ongoing story during November that vividly illustrated this violence and its resultant intimidation. About three a.m. on Sunday, November 5, fifty-two hours before voting places opened in rural Ouachita Parish and only months after the Cruikshank and Reese decisions, a posse of hooded white men knocked down the door of Henry Pinkston's cabin, dragged him from bed, and shot him several times. Next they beat and shot his wife, Eliza, and cut their baby's throat from ear to ear and threw the body into a nearby pond. Why? Henry Pinkston was a colored man known throughout the parish as a "steadfast and . . . demonstrative Republican."[22] The tale could be told because Eliza miraculously survived. According to contemporary accounts, there were 2,107 Republican voters in the parish; "only 781 went to the polls on election day."[23] In Florida the initial count showed 24,337 for Hayes and 24,294 for Tilden, leaving a Republican majority of 43.

Until the states' election boards, called returning boards, verified all votes, nothing was official. Republicans controlled the boards in all three states: South Carolina, with seven Republican members including three who were themselves running for office (thereby supervising their own election returns); Louisiana, with four Republican members; and Florida, with two Republicans and one Democrat. Since new federal troops reinforced those already present, the National Democratic Party saw little chance for a fair canvass of the returns. For this reason Hewitt asked several prominent Democrats and Republicans to head south to observe the tabulating process. President Grant sent additional Republican watchdogs.

The Constitution prescribed that registered voters cast their ballots not for Hayes or Tilden, but for a slate of electors representing each man. Once the state officials had tallied and approved the popular vote, the electors of the slate that had received the most votes were certified as duly elected. The Constitution also required all electors to cast their votes on the same day, the first Wednesday in December, which in 1876 was December 6, and send the results to the president of the Senate in Washington. Normally, the vice president, who presides over the Senate and who votes only in the case of tie, is the president of the Senate. Because Vice President Wilson died in 1875, the Senate selected Senator Thomas Ferry of Michigan to be president pro tempore, or temporary president.

In South Carolina the Board of Canvassers consisted of the secretary of state, comptroller general, attorney general, auditor, treasurer, and inspector general, plus a seventh nonvoting member. All were Republican, three were Negroes, and the three whites were candidates in the election. The board had the power to canvass returns for everyone except the governor and the lieutenant governor, whose elections were determined by a joint session of the legislature. The board decided all cases under protest. How could the Republicans lose under these conditions, Manton Marble and other Northern Democrats who were on hand asked. Marble wired Pelton about various Republican affidavits that proved fraudulent, but no matter. On December 6 the electors met and cast seven ballots for Hayes and

Wheeler, which were certified and forwarded to Washington. The Democratic electoral claimants also met on December 6 and hurried their seven votes for Tilden and Hendricks to the president of the Senate.

In Louisiana, the foremost center of contention, the returning board by law should have consisted of five men, at least one of whom was required to be a member of the minority party. The only Democrat had resigned two years earlier, yet the Republican majority had consistently refused to fill the vacancy. Former governor James Madison Wells, T. C. Anderson of Opelousas, freedman Louis M. Kenner, and Gadane Casanave, a free man of color before the war, constituted the board. When sheriff of Rapides Parish, Wells had embezzled over $12,000 in tax monies. A Unionist during the Civil War, he was elected governor in 1864 only to be removed by Gen. Philip Sheridan when military reconstruction began two years later. Sheridan characterized his conduct as "sinuous as the mark left in the dust by the movement of a snake."[24] "Mad" Wells presided over the four-man board. The other white man was Thomas L. Anderson, a state senator who had siphoned public money into a navigation company he partly owned. Louis Kenner owned a bad-reputation saloon adjacent to the State House and at one time had been indicted for larceny. Cassanave, an undertaker by trade, was probably the only honest member of the board, but he was not thought very bright. All were native-born Louisianans. Not only was the returning board partisan, so too were many of the visiting "statesmen." Senator John Sherman, for example, assured Hayes that Wells was "thoroughly honest and conscientious."[25]

"Within a week [of the election] the St. Charles Hotel [in New Orleans] might have been mistaken for a caravansary of the national Capital," Democratic watchdog Henry Watterson wrote.[26] Twenty-six Republicans, among them John Sherman, Stanley Matthews, James Garfield, and William Evarts, and twenty-five Democrats, including Watterson, former Liberal Republican Lyman Trumbull, and Speaker of the House Samuel J. Randall, descended upon the port city.[27] "New Orleans was new to most of the 'visiting statesmen,'" Watterson continued, "and we attended the places of amusement, lived in the restaurants, and saw the sights as if we had been tourists in a foreign land and not just partisans charged with the business of adjusting a Presidential election from implacable points of view."

The surface friendliness and "certain degree of personal intimacy," as Watterson described their restaurant camaraderie, notwithstanding, Watterson wired Tilden to speak out, to do something, as "the conspiracy of a few men to use the corrupt returning boards of Louisiana, South Carolina, and Florida to upset the election

. . . might by prompt exposure and popular appeal be thwarted." Nor was Watterson the only Democrat to implore Tilden to arouse public opinion—but still no reaction from Gramercy Park. On November 13 Watterson once more prevailed upon Tilden to at least speak to Hayes about joint measures to secure a fair count. Others, including Mississippi representative L. Q. C. Lamar and Pennsylvanian representative Samuel Randall joined Watterson in this appeal. Despite innumerable similar requests from all over the country, Tilden initiated no appeal to Hayes, gave no encouragement to embattled Southerners, and made no attempt to dramatize the Democratic position before the public. The *New York Tribune* aptly commented that the party was "in the position of an army waiting for orders from its general," but no orders came.[28] Despite his disgust ("My spirit was depressed and my confidence discouraged by the intense quietude on our side.") Watterson stayed in New Orleans.[29]

The returning board began its deliberations as soon as the returns had been re-ported. As the New Orleans *Daily Picayune* put it, "The problem upon which they are engaged is how to elect the Republican candidates with a Democratic majority. They have done it before and they will do it again."[30] After concluding its public hearings, the board held several days of secret deliberations.

"Corruption was in the air," Watterson wrote.[31] He believed, he said, that the reason for the secret meetings was to buy time for the members to sell their votes. Soon he himself was approached by a well-known state senator. As if he were pro-posing to dispose of a horse or dog, he stated his errand:

> "You think you can deliver the goods," said I.
> "I am authorized to make the offer," he answered.
> "And for how much?" I asked.
> "Two hundred and fifty thousand dollars," he replied. "One hundred thou-sand each for Wells and Anderson, and twenty-five thousand apiece for the niggers."

Watterson took their exchange as a joke, so he glibly replied, "Senator . . . the terms are cheap as dirt. I don't happen to have the amount about me at the mo-ment, but I will communicate with my principal and see you later." Watterson promptly forgot the episode until the same state senator showed up later in the St. Charles lobby and pressed him for the money. Only then did Watterson realize the offer of a bribe had been real.

Hewitt, who kept careful records and notes of all that transpired around him, wrote,

> I had it from the mouth of Governor Wells himself that the offer rejected by the Democrats had been accepted by the Republican managers, and that they had agreed after the inauguration of President Hayes to raise the money to pay the amount in cash. In consequence of the failure to redeem this promise, Governor Wells subsequently came to Washington and threatened to expose the whole transaction. Whereupon, as I was informed on good authority, a considerable portion of the money was raised and paid over to Wells in Washington in order to quiet the immediate clamor; with the promise that the remainder should be paid in time. Whether it was paid or not I do not know. Possibly Wells was quieted by his appointment to the office of Collector of Customs for the Port of New Orleans; his confederates were also provided for, some by offices and some by money.[32]

Bribing went on in Florida as well, at least to the extent revealed by the aptly named cipher telegrams.[33] Shortly after the election the Western Union Company delivered 30,000 telegrams to Congress that had been sent by members of both parties during the campaign. By some as-yet-unrevealed sleight, the Republican dispatches were returned to Western Union and burned, but Republican leaders secretly retained 750 telegrams, some of which were in cipher, sent by Democrats. The cipher telegrams were given to the *New York Tribune*, whose staff deciphered them.[34] They revealed messages between Manton Marble and William Pelton trying to consummate a deal. For $200,000 the Democrats could have Florida. Too high, Pelton cried. Marble telegraphed a revised quotation of $50,000, to which Pelton agreed. Neither Hewitt nor Tilden had any knowledge of Pelton's attempted malfeasance. In any case, time ran out before the deal could be completed.

Finally, circumstantial evidence suggested chicanery on the part of Charles Farwell, a Republican visiting observer, in Louisiana. He assured Hayes's friend William Henry Smith that there was no need to worry: "The vote cast, illegal and legal combined as you are aware, is against us, but I have no reason today to fear the result. I am in constant communication with those who know and they assure me that all will be well."[35] Much later Smith reminded Hayes that Farwell "in all delicate and important matters last year . . . was our right hand man" and that "his wealth . . . supplied the means when no other could be reached."

On December 5 the board announced its final tally. It rejected 13,250 Democratic votes and 2,040 Republican votes, thereby converting Tilden majorities of 6,300 to 8,900 into Hayes majorities of 4,600 to 4,700. On December 6 both Republican and Democratic electors met separately, voted, and forwarded their results to Washington. When the Republican certificate reached Washington, president pro tempore Ferry noticed improper endorsements on the envelope, so the Hayes electors had to reconvene and fill out another certificate, which they antedated December 6. Since two electors did not make the second electoral meeting, their signatures were forged. As a result, Louisiana submitted three sets of votes to Washington.

The Florida returning board consisted of two Republicans and one Democrat, all three white Southerners. Although state law required the board to begin its work as soon as returns were received, it kept delaying going to work. Democrats demanded action and when nothing happened went to court to get an order that the canvassing proceed. The board started work November 27. Another state election law permitted voters to cast their ballots at any of the polls in the county where they lived, a statute designed to give Negroes the option of voting at the county seat where they were provided protection. The practice, however, made repeat voting easy and fairly undetectable. Democrats accused Republican county officials of altering the Archer precinct returns in Alachua County by adding 219 fraudulent Republican votes. President Grant asked Francis Barlow, a former Union general, to investigate and defend the Republican case at Archer precinct. As a New York attorney general who had assisted Tilden in sending Boss Tweed to jail, Barlow was disgusted by what he witnessed. Very quickly he concluded that the Democrats had a better claim in Alachua County than his own party. He reported his findings to William E. Chandler, who was busy keeping his eye on all three returning boards. Chandler promptly removed Barlow from the case and replaced him with Edward F. Noyes. Noyes asked Republican chairman of the county, L. G. Dennis, to take the stand, but Dennis refused. If he had to speak under oath, he told Noyes, he would have to admit that the Republicans had submitted fraudulent votes and that, in fact, the Democrats had taken the county. Despite these findings, the board promptly accepted the Alachua return as it was, a Republican victory.

Gen. Lew Wallace of Indiana, the future author of *Ben Hur*, also went to Florida as a Republican watchdog, and like Barlow, he deplored what he saw. He wrote his wife,

Money and intimidation can obtain the oath of white men as well as black to any required statement. A ton of affidavits could be carted into the state house tomorrow, and not a word of truth in them, except the names of the parties swearing, and their ages and places of residence. Now what can come of such a state of things? If we win, our methods are subject to impeachment for possible fraud. If the enemy win, it is the same thing exactly—doubt, suspicion, irritation go with the consequence, whatever it may be.[36]

On December 6 the Republican electors met and cast their votes for Hayes and Wheeler. At the same time attorneys for Tilden applied to the circuit court for a writ of *quo warranto* requiring the Hayes electors to show cause why they should not be replaced by Democratic electors. Even though ample precedent existed for judicial intervention in Florida elections, the electors went ahead and completed their certificate and dispatched their four votes to Senator Ferry. Even if the state supreme court accepted a case against them, they reasoned, the federal courts would surely step in on their behalf. State attorney general J. P. Cocke, therefore, issued a certificate of election to the Democratic electors who met the same day, cast their four votes for Tilden and Hendricks, and sent their certificates to Washington. When the new Democratic governor George Drew was inaugurated on New Year's Day, thus ending reconstruction in Florida, he and the new Democratic legislature ordered a second canvass of presidential votes that favored Tilden. A law quickly passed that directed the governor to certify these votes, which he did. So, for the second time in the nation's history, a third set of votes from a single state went to Senator Ferry.

For an antidote to the "fraud thus perpetrated," Hewitt looked to Oregon. No one disputed a Hayes majority of a thousand votes, but the Constitution clearly stated federal officeholders cannot act as electors, and one of the Oregon electors was a postmaster. The state's Democratic governor refused his certificate and gave it to the next highest vote-getter, a Tilden elector. As a result, Tilden got his necessary 185 electoral votes to become president. Hewitt saw this turn of events as a lucky opportunity. He knew that in at least one of the Southern states the Republicans had thrown out enough Democratic votes through the returning board to give Hayes the electors. He also knew that no federal authority had the right to go behind official state returns. Hewitt figured that by insisting on the Oregon governor's right to go to the Tilden elector, he could force the Republicans in Washington to go behind the returns. If they went behind Oregon's returns, he surmised, how could they refuse to go behind them in South Carolina, Louisiana, and Florida. Oregon also sent two sets of electors to Washington, thereby magnifying the electoral madness Congress would have to straighten out.

Thirty-four states, as the Constitution stipulated, sent one set of results to Washington that showed Tilden had 184 electoral votes of the needed 185, and Hayes had 165. Both candidates claimed the remaining twenty votes, nineteen of which belonged to three Southern states and the other to Oregon. Clearly a political battle lay ahead, prompting many to do what they could to protect their side. One such man was Col. W. H. Roberts, editor of the *New Orleans Times*. According to the *New York Herald*, Roberts met with Governor Hayes in Columbus for three hours. The gist of Roberts's message, that Southern leaders were not averse to a Hayes presidency *if* they were left alone to manage their own affairs, Hayes readily accepted. According to Roberts, Hayes said "that carpetbag governments had not been successful; that the complaints of the Southern people were just in this matter. . . . If inaugurated, he would insist on, he said, absolute justice and fair play to the Negro," and believed "this could be got best and most surely by trusting the honorable and influential southern whites."[37]

As a newspaperman himself, Roberts had no reluctance to supply details of the interview to the press. Northern Democrats and Radical Republicans were furious. Reporters questioned Hayes about the meeting, but he refused to talk about the matter. The furor did not subside. On December 6 Hayes wrote Attorney General Alphonso Taft, calling the story a fabrication, yet a few days later in Cincinnati he admitted that Southern Democrats had been in touch with him with assurances of their good will and cooperation.

Tilden looked like the only citizen removed from the churning controversy. Deep in his law books, he and John Bigelow examined statutes and precedents for counting electoral votes. Even after Blaine told Bigelow that Republicans would have backed down if Tilden had been firm, he remained silent. Hewitt, however, would not give up. To incite some response from Tilden, he asked Allen G. Thurman, Democratic senator from Ohio and a man who had the confidence of his party, to stop in New York on his way to Washington for the closing session of the 44th Congress. Thurman conferred with Tilden and got right to the point. "We can fight; we can back down; or we can arbitrate." Tilden replied, "It will not do to fight. We have just emerged from one Civil War, and it will never do to engage in another . . . it would end in the destruction of free government. We cannot back down. We can, therefore, only arbitrate."[38] The questions Hewitt and Thurman were left with as they made their way to Washington were how, with whom, and under whose authority could, or should, they arbitrate.

Hewitt decided he had to get Grant's reading on the situation before he tried to figure out what to do. He got an appointment that Secretary of State Hamilton Fish arranged to see the president on December 3. After their meeting Hewitt dictated to a stenographer an account of their conversation. He had two copies made and sent one to President Grant with a request that he correct any errors. The president made no corrections.

During the meeting Grant spoke about all three Southern states, but only when he got to Louisiana did he ask Hewitt to keep what he said in confidence.

He said that on the face of the returns, Tilden and Hendricks unquestionably had a majority of six to eight thousand votes; that there were six parishes in which there had been intimidation to such an extent that he did not think there had been a fair election, and that they had to be thrown out; that he believed that when thrown out, there was still a majority for Tilden and Hendricks, to which I remarked that it was somewhere about two thousand, and that this majority could only be overcome by assuming that the votes of five thousand naturalized citizens of New Orleans were all Democratic, and that by throwing them out on account of some defect in the naturalization papers. The President remarked that the returning board in Louisiana was in very bad odor with the public; that the people had no confidence in it, and even if it did right, it would not be credited with honest intentions. He believed that there had been no honest election in Louisiana since Slidell [Senator John Slidell, Democrat of Louisiana] got control of its politics.

I suggested to him that, as a matter of fact, it was not possible to have a fair election in that state, and that it was a most serious blow to Republican government that a state in which a fair election could not be had, should decide a presidential contest.

The President replied that this was true, and that it would not be unreasonable that the vote of Louisiana should be thrown out, as it was in 1872, on account of irregularities of election, and the peculiar functions of the returning board.[39]

Of course if Louisiana's vote were thrown out, the election, as both Grant and Hewitt knew, would go to the House, as the Constitution requires. Since the House was Democratic, Tilden would become president.

The 1876 presidential drama moved its main stage from the deep South to Washington as the 44th Congress convened during the first week of December. On day one of the session the House provided for three committees to visit South Carolina, Louisiana, and Florida. The next day the Senate directed its Committee on Elections to examine returns in six Southern states and in Oregon. These inquiries provided no answers toward resolution. During the remainder of the month all sorts of suggestions were made. Why not hold another national election, for example? No, answered the Republicans, for they were sure Tilden would carry the country. Why not a new election in the three contested Southern states? No, again from the Republicans, who believed such a reelection would produce several Tilden electors, and he only needed one. Finally, a Republican from Iowa introduced a resolution in the House calling on Speaker Randall to appoint a committee to act in concert with a similar committee to be appointed in the Senate that would prepare a bill or a constitutional amendment to solve the electoral enigma. Both houses agreed and just before Christmas recess Speaker Randall and Senator Ferry named the two committees.

A mere eleven years after the cataclysmic Civil War, the country faced an abstruse crisis that begged for all the celebrated American genius for compromise. But how to compromise when the Constitution was maddeningly ambiguous as to how the validity of the disputed returns should be decided? The Twelfth Amendment directed the president of the Senate to open electoral certificates in the presence of both houses: "The votes shall then be counted." The Constitution said nothing about what to do when more than one set of votes is submitted by a state.

The year of America's centennial ended in stalemate and in frustration of the popular will. In two short months President Grant must be packed and out of the White House, but who would move in absorbed not only Congress but also the whole country.

WE, THE OTHER PEOPLE

*T*he United States had survived for a hundred years, growing from a federation of thirteen colonies along the Atlantic seaboard to a vast continental nation—amazing, given its ideological divide between states' sovereignty and union supremacy. And now an unresolved presidential election threatened once again to tear it apart. The Civil War, a mere eleven years earlier, had almost dealt a killing blow. Yet even before Ulysses Grant had assumed command of the Union armies in March 1864, a college professor from Indiana suggested a centennial celebration honoring the one hundredth anniversary of American independence in 1776.[1] At a Smithsonian conference marking the three hundredth anniversary of Galileo's birth, Wabash College professor John L. Campbell urged the federal government to organize an international exhibition for the nation's centennial.

Five long years elapsed before Congress endorsed his idea, and even then it refused to allocate funds. The March 3, 1871, act that established an "International Exhibition of Arts, Manufactures, and Products of Soil and Mine, in the City of Philadelphia" stated that "the United States shall not be liable for any expenses attending such an exhibition."[2] By the time a Centennial Board of Finance had been created to raise capital by selling stock to the public, a depression gripped the United States in an economic slump that would last straight through the six months of the exhibition. The act also set up a Centennial Commission with commissioners nominated by the governors and appointed by the president from every state and territory. The commission chose a site, Fairmount Park, at nearly three thousand acres one of the largest city parks in the nation; fixed the opening and closing dates, May 10 to November 10, 1876; and elected Alfred Goshorn, a manufacturer of white lead from Cincinnati, as director of the exhibition. Secretary of State Fish dispatched official invitations to every foreign government to participate. When thirty-seven nations accepted,[3] Congress, belatedly and reluctantly, approved a $1.5 million loan to supplement money raised privately. Astonishingly, two hundred and forty-nine buildings, with almost one hundred acres of floor space under roof, and holding more than thirty thousand exhibits, had been erected and opened on schedule, free of debt.

The main Exhibition Hall, 1,880 feet long and 464 feet wide, was the largest building on the fairgrounds, covering more than 20 acres. Three thousand workmen installed 4 miles of pipe, hauled 8.5 million pounds of iron, and hammered 7 million feet of lumber to provide space for 13,720 American and foreign exhibits.

Nearby Machinery Hall was to become the fair's leading attraction because of its mighty Corliss steam engine, named for designer George H. Corliss of Providence, Rhode Island.[4] Weighing 700 tons, it rose 40 feet into the air, generated 1,600 horsepower, and had a 56-ton flywheel that revolved without noise because the machine's sole operator worked in a separate building with twenty steam boilers. The Corliss drove 8,000 machines—lathes, saws, drills, looms, presses, and pumps that spun cotton, printed newspapers, made envelopes, lithographed wallpaper, sewed fabric, sawed and shaped wood, and pumped water. In short, the Corliss was a powerful sign that machines were the country's future.

The third largest building, Agricultural Hall, provided nine acres of an enormous variety of food and fiber from every climate. The art gallery, called Memorial Hall, a massive granite building surmounted by a dome of glass, displayed 3,256 paintings and drawings, 627 sculptures, photographs, and numerous examples of applied art. As the first international art show ever held in the United States, the building and its collection launched an era of museum expansion throughout the nation. Up to the time of its construction, the country had only three museums, one at Yale University, another in nearby Hartford, Connecticut, and a third, the Corcoran Gallery, in Washington, D.C.

Horticultural Hall, the largest conservatory hothouse in the world but the smallest of the Centennial's five principal buildings, was thought to be the most beautiful structure of the exhibition. Of Moorish design, it seemed to float above a reflecting pool and surrounding flowerbeds. Other buildings included a cross-shaped United States Government Building, twenty-four state buildings, and a Women's Pavilion.

In the face of the continuing economic depression with millions of workers unemployed, fair planners worried that no one would come to view the wonders they had assembled. But come they did. Ten million visitors descended upon Philadelphia. The country's second largest city had 800,000 inhabitants crowded into a narrow strip of land lying between the Schuylkill and Delaware Rivers. Although American families traveled little or not at all, one out of every five Americans came, and from all parts of the nation. Henry Ford's father, William, was one of these travelers, his first big trip since he had left Ireland twenty-nine years before. When he returned to Dearborn, William Ford's description of what he had seen—the mighty Corliss, the typewriter that "supercedes the pen,"[5] various refrigeration processes, Fleischmann's Yeast, a new "floor-cloth" called linoleum, the telephone, and the band saw that carpenters all over America would use to curlicue and decorate Victorian houses—opened up to thirteen-year-old Henry the exciting possibilities of the emerging machine age.

The Centennial also brought to America for the first time a large number of foreign visitors, government officials, businessmen, technical experts, reporters, and even tourists. The best known of these visitors, Emperor Dom Pedro II of Brazil, who, with his wife, the Empress Theresa, were the first reigning monarchs ever to visit the United States.[6] People in the South were already familiar with the emperor. Although monarch of the country with the largest slave population in the world, Dom Pedro was opposed to slavery, freeing all the slaves he had himself inherited. Yet believing Southern planters had much to teach Brazilian farmers, at the end of the Civil War he encouraged defeated Confederates to settle in Brazil. To this end, he provided free transportation to Rio de Janeiro, cheap land in the fertile São Paulo region, and free provisions during initial settlement. Since neither records were kept nor were passports required, no one knows how many embittered Confederates, called *Confederados* by the Portuguese-speaking Brazilians, had moved to Brazil, but estimates range from three to twenty thousand. Those who did emigrate prospered and remained, as Confederates who left their native land after the war for Mexico, Central America, and Venezuela had not. The emperor's helping hand had made the difference.

At the time the exhibition opened, this descendant of the Houses of Bourbon, Braganza, and Hapsburg had become exceedingly popular with North Americans.

Dom Pedro II arrived in New York City on April 15. Early in May he went to Washington, where he called on President Grant, trekked through the Smithsonian, viewed the paintings in the Corcoran, listened to a day of the Senate's impeachment hearings against Secretary of War Belknap, visited the unfinished Washington Monument, met his military hero General Sherman, and dined several times at Wormley's hotel. When he appeared May 10 on the platform with President Grant in Philadelphia to hear the premiere performance of "Centennial March" composed by Richard Wagner and commissioned by the Women's Centennial Committee for the opening ceremonies, scarcely a person in the country had not heard or read about the emperor.

The women's committee paid Wagner five thousand dollars for his march, and in light of their treatment by the Centennial managers, their donation was generous to a fault. In 1873 the Centennial Board of Finance had appointed thirteen local women to a special women's committee and told them to elect Elizabeth Duane Gillespie as their president. Mrs. Gillespie then organized committees in states across the land to raise money and to scout for exhibits that would be shown in the Main Building. But eleven months before the opening, the Centennial management told Mrs. Gillespie that because of the higher-than-expected number of foreign countries planning to exhibit, the resulting "struggle for space" left no room for the women.[7] Told to finance and build their own building, Mrs. Gillespie raised the money in record time, commissioned a one-acre pavilion, and organized the exhibits, all of which were made and operated by women, including several inventions that lessened domestic labor like a meat tenderizer, a machine for washing blankets, another for washing and drying dishes, and a mangle for ironing bedsheets. A young girl operated a steam engine to run a press that printed a daily journal, the *New Century for Women*.

Because most Americans believed that the women's rights movement threatened the notion that women's work should be confined to the home, Mrs. Gillespie was quoted in the *New York Times* as declaring that no "person [must] confound the character of this institution [women's pavilion] with women's rights, because they are as far asunder as poles."[8] Suffragettes, however, disagreed. In addition to recognition of their talents, women, they insisted, wanted full citizenship rights. Accordingly, Susan B. Anthony, Elizabeth Cady Stanton, and Matilda Gage, leaders of the national Women's Suffrage Association, asked for permission from the president of the Centennial Commission to present such a request at the Fourth of July celebration to Senator Thomas Ferry, standing in for President Grant. Their

Wormley's Hotel opened in December 1871 with seventy-four rooms near Lafayette Square and the White House.

Courtesy of Kiplinger Research Library, the Historical Society of Washington, D.C.

James Wormley (1819–1884), portrait by Henry Ulke.
Courtesy of Kiplinger Research Library, the Historical Society of Washington, D.C.

ALEXANDER R. SHEPHERD, GOVERNOR OF THE DISTRICT OF COLUMBIA.—PHOTOGRAPHED BY
HENRY ULKE & BRO., WASHINGTON, D. C.

Alexander Shepherd (1835–1902) is credited with turning shabby D.C.
into the country's best lighted and paved city in the early 1870s.
Courtesy of Kiplinger Research Library, the Historical Society of Washington, D.C.

"Brains of Tammany," a cartoon by Thomas Nast of *Harper's Weekly* depicting William "Boss" Tweed (1823–1878). *Courtesy of the Rutherford B. Hayes Presidential Center*

Rutherford B. Hayes (1822–1893) on "Louisiana donkey"; Samuel Tilden (1814–1886) on ground. *Courtesy of the Rutherford B. Hayes Presidential Center*

Rutherford B. Hayes in 1879, during his presidency.
Courtesy of the Rutherford B. Hayes Presidential Center

Ulysses Grant (1822–1885) was president from 1869 to 1877.
Courtesy of the Rutherford B. Hayes Presidential Center

Samuel Tilden defeated Hayes in the popular vote in 1876.
Courtesy of the Rutherford B. Hayes Presidential Center

repudiation resulted in more drastic action on their part. While seated in the audience listening to a reading of the Declaration of Independence, five women, pushing past generals and governors, made their way to the platform, handed their declaration of rights to Senator Ferry, then distributed copies of their protest as Anthony read the declaration aloud. She protested taxation without representation, unequal legal codes for men and women, and asserted that "universal manhood suffrage, by establishing an aristocracy of sex, imposes upon women of this nation, a more absolute and cruel despotism than monarchy."[9] "A very discourteous interruption," summed up the press.[10]

When word reached Philadelphia of the massacre of Gen. George Custer and his band of 250 soldiers by Sioux warriors led by Sitting Bull and Crazy Horse on July 6, all suffragette stories disappeared from newspapers. Custer, against orders, made a direct frontal assault on several thousand Cheyennes and Sioux in the Bighorn River region of southern Montana. The Indians killed Custer's force to the last soldier, including George Custer's younger brother Thomas, on June 25, 1876. The story did not reach the newspapers back East until July. Their writers gave highly romanticized version of "Custer's Last Stand," namely that brave soldiers had been massacred by bloodthirsty Indians, when in fact they had been defending lands reserved for them by an 1868 treaty. The sad truth about "Custer's Last Stand" was broken government promises. The battle should have been called the Indians' Last Stand because it marked their last successful act of resistance against the white man, who henceforth was never again challenged, leading to the extinction of the singular way of Indian life.

After the Battle of Little Bighorn, fair visitors flocked to the exhibit of Indian artifacts the Smithsonian had collected and displayed in 8,000 of its allotted 26,600 square feet in the U.S. Government Building.[11] A few dedicated individuals, led by Spencer Baird of the Smithsonian, had collected the artifacts. Because the congressional mandate specified that goods collected for the display be turned over to the Smithsonian for permanent display in Washington after the Centennial, Baird managed to get money from the office of Indian affairs to fund ethnological expeditions to areas in Alaska and the West. The moccasins, pottery, tomahawks, canoes, coup sticks, jewelry, snowshoes, dog sleds, totem poles, and wigwams illustrated something of the Indian past, but the contrived picturesqueness of the exhibit hid the sad state of the Indian present, and made the point that Indians represented the antithesis of progress. Mannequins with frightening-looking papier-mâché faces and garments hung on wire skeletons, like that of Red

Cloud, chief of the Dakota Sioux, shown as "repulsive looking" with raised tom-ahawk and belt of human scalps, led fairgoers to make unfair judgments.[12] Never mind that Red Cloud in real life was handsome and friendly toward the government, the display led even so intelligent an observer as William Dean Howells, editor of the *Atlantic Monthly*, to remark, "The red man, as he appears in effigy and photo in this collection is a hideous demon, whose malign traits can hardly inspire any emotion softer than abhorrence. . . . In blaming our Indian agents for malfeasance in office, perhaps we do not sufficiently account for the demoralizing influence of merely beholding those false and pitiless savage faces; moldy flour and corrupt beef seem altogether too good for them."[13]

A sufficient number of real-life Indians on the fairgrounds might have undercut negative responses like that of Howells, but few Indians got to Philadelphia, and not for lack of trying. A number of tribal leaders had asked to participate. Several chiefs of Missouri tribes, for example, asked permission to leave their reservations saying, "We have many friends in Philadelphia that we wish to shake hands with."[14] They also wanted to stop off in Washington to see the president because he had not answered their letters. Indian commissioner John Q. Smith responded to a number of these appeals, but apparently not to any from Missouri: "Cannot authorize absence of any Indians from their reservation. If you are satisfied, and will be responsible that Menomenees [a peaceful tribe living on a reservation in northeastern Wisconsin] will go as visitors only in charge of competent and proper persons, will not discredit themselves or the Indian service and will return without expense of government, I will not object."[15] As a result, a small Indian encampment lived on the fairgrounds under the supervision of the well-known Texas scout and fighter of Indians, George Anderson.

Spencer Baird tried to bring about a more substantial Indian presence. He drew up a list of tribes he wanted to invite and devised a checklist for tribal representatives to use in choosing participants.[16] Individuals selected had to be more white than Indian, influential with the tribe, speak English, be pleasant, clean, good-looking, and bring a clean child, dog, and pony. That compliance with such a list negated any attempt to present authentic native culture seemed lost on Baird. But despite feverish attempts to get money from Congress to support the chosen Indians at subsistence level for six months in Philadelphia, including even an appeal from President Grant, Congress refused money and so ended the possibility of further Indian participation.

As unfairly as women and Native Americans were treated, at least some had been asked to take part in the nation's official centennial, which contrasted sharply with the neglect accorded Negroes. Yet people of color encouraged their own people to participate. As early as March 1872 an individual who identified himself only as Brister wrote a letter to the editor of the *Christian Recorder*, the weekly put out by the African Methodist Episcopal (A.M.E.) Church. Because of the unrecognized military service, inventions, discoveries, and uncompensated toil made by Negroes, he urged his people to "claim that our labor of the past had added something to the glory of the country."[17] Eighteen months later Benjamin Tanner, director of the *Christian Recorder*, responded to Brister's letter by appealing to Negroes to act. "As a people we are surely to be credited with as much . . . patriotism as the alien Romanists [immigrant Catholics who were planning to erect on the Centennial grounds an elaborate fountain], who are not and cannot be truly American."[18] After this nativist outburst, he urged that a bronze statue of Richard Allen, first bishop of the A.M.E. church, be raised on the fairgrounds.

Other Negroes spoke out as well. Robert Purvis, a colored abolitionist and civil rights advocate from Philadelphia, reasoned that once whites understood how patriotically and bravely African Americans had served on the battlefields of the Revolutionary War, the War of 1812, and the Civil War, color prejudice would vanish. Negro congressman Josiah T. Walls from Florida urged Congress to appropriate $3 million to put on what he saw as a "patriotic demonstration of a hundred years of popular government . . . [and of] a free people at their unbroken union and the restored unity of their nationality."[19] Frederick Douglass agreed and encouraged Negroes across the country to work toward their representation at the event. The convention of colored newspaper men in 1875 appointed a Centennial committee to contract for a statue by African American Edmonia Lewis, noted for her striking, emotional portrayal of women and slaves in sculpture, and to oversee the publication of an eighteen-volume history of the Negro.

Exposition directors pretty much ignored these calls to action, although the women's committee had asked Negro women to help raise funds by selling stock subscriptions. At the first organizational meeting, the colored women discovered that their work was to be confined to persons of their color. When they protested, the white women passed a resolution that conferred an "honorable discharge." Negative publicity ensued, forcing the white women to issue an apology and to promise not to discriminate racially. Accordingly, the colored women resumed fundraising, but never received recognition nor exhibit space in the Women's Pavilion.

At a Centennial fundraiser in 1874 put on by the Philadelphia police at the Arch Street Theatre, Pusey A. Peer and his wife arrived at the theater with their paid-for tickets. The police refused admittance, hurling racist slurs. "Throw the niggers out," the police shouted as they forcibly ejected them from the theater, injuring them in the processs.[20]

No matter how much they tried to be a part of the national celebration, colored Americans in the end had no exhibit they could call their own. The only exhibit that directly related to their heritage, a statue, *The Freed Slave*, also called *The Abolition of Slavery in the United States*, was not even an American exhibit. Francesco Pezzicar, an Austrian of Italian descent, produced a bronze man standing half-naked on a pedestal, arms outstretched, holding in one hand a crumpled sheet signifying the Emancipation Proclamation. His broken chains rest between his bare feet, and he clearly revels in his newly granted freedom. William Dean Howells described the statue as "a most offensive Frenchy Negro who has broken his chain, and spreading both his arms and legs abroad is rioting in a declaration of something—one longs to clap him back into hopeless bondage."[21]

The only representations of the work of American Negro artists were Edmonia Lewis's sculpture, *The Death of Cleopatra*, Edward Bannister's painting, *Under the Oaks*, and a painting by Robert Duncanson. Lewis's two-ton statue became the most talked about piece at the exposition. The Egyptian queen is shown seated in a chair with her head dropping over her left shoulder and an asp in her hand. *Under the Oaks*, an oil depiction of a herd of sheep along the branch of a creek with a hill and trees in the background, won an award.

The proposed statue of Richard Allen, first A.M.E. bishop, was erected in Fairmont Park, but not until November 2, only eight days before the Centennial Exposition closed on November 10. From the first, A.M.E. church organizers squabbled with exposition organizers. The Methodists wanted to erect a permanent monument. The organizers provided space for the Allen statue on condition that it be removed within sixty days of the fair's close. Only when the Bethel Philadelphia congregation offered a permanent place for the statue did the A.M.E. organizers proceed. They chose Negro artist Alfred White of Ohio to sculpt a life-sized marble bust of Bishop Allen. For the pedestal on which the bust would sit organizers chose an artist who resided in Italy, probably Edmonia Lewis, who lived in Rome at the time.

The dedication of the monument site in Fairmount Park took place on June 22, more than six weeks after the exposition had opened. Reverend John Jennifer of the A.M.E. Arkansas conference spoke powerfully, linking African Americans with their ancient lineage by calling attention to that first human impulse to commemorate, namely the pyramids of Egypt. "How becoming it is for us, the children of ancestors who were the founders of the earliest civilization," he said, to join "this feast of nations in this our own beloved country at this her first centennial feast."[22] His words undercut the dominant message of white history and white sectional reconciliation being proclaimed everywhere else in Fairmount Park. Not once mentioning Richard Allen, Jennifer spoke of black labor in the South since the seventeenth century, criticized the nation's tolerance of the Ku Klux Klan and White Leagues, and hoped to see color lines wiped out. In short, Jennifer used this opportunity to speak out to the large racially mixed audience in order to redefine the story of Negroes' bondage as a story of nation building. The actual unveiling of the statue, he announced, would not take place until September 22, the anniversary of the publication of Lincoln's Emancipation Proclamation.

"Having labored during almost the whole of my political life for the emancipation and enfranchisement of your race," Rutherford Hayes wrote from Columbus, Ohio, on September 12, "I feel a special interest in the occasion."[23] He did not, however, attend. It was just as well, since the September 22 event had to be postponed yet again. During transport from Cincinnati to Philadelphia, the entire pedestal was lost in a railroad accident. A new pedestal was made, and on Thursday, November 2, the statue was unveiled; the Allen monument was the first erected in this country by colored Americans to honor one of their own.

Other than these few paintings and sculptures, as well as examination papers of students attending Southern schools including Negro students, and an oil painting of jubilee singers of Fisk University, the exclusion of Negroes was nearly total. They were even barred from the construction crews that built the exhibition halls, despite an unemployment rate of 70 percent among Philadelphia's Negroes. Once the fair opened a few colored men did find employment as waiters, hotel clerks, messengers, janitors, and as performers at a concession called the Southern Restaurant. Edward Mercer, a white businessman from Atlanta, owned the Southern Restaurant and provided a description of it for the fair's guidebook. "A band of old-time plantation 'darkies' will sing their quaint melodies and strum the banjo before visitors of every clime. . . . Imagine the phlegmatic German exhibitor with his 'frau and kinder' gazing with astonishment at the pure and unadulterated 'essence of Ole Virginny' expounded by a hand from the cotton field, or solemn-visaged Turk receiving with ill-concealed horror, a dusky son of Tophet 'rattling of the bones.'"[24] In other words, newly freed slaves were happy, carefree, and childlike. The harsh realities of lynching and sharecropping were not mentioned.

Nor was there any mention when a bale of former slave Benjamin Montgomery's cotton won an agricultural medal, defeating entries from all over the South, Brazil, Egypt, and the Fiji Islands. Davis Bend, Mississippi, where Benjamin Montgomery grew his prize cotton, contained the huge plantations of Jefferson Davis and his brother Joseph. Before the war the Davis brothers had tried to set up a model Negro community; they fed and housed their slaves better than other planters throughout the state and they allowed them a degree of self-government, including a slave jury system that enforced plantation discipline. By the time Union troops arrived in 1863, Joseph Davis had fled, leaving his Negroes to run the plantation. In 1864 the entire area was set aside for the exclusive settlement of freedmen. When the idea of the Freedmen's Bureau actively promoting property ownership by Negroes came to an abrupt end, the land reverted to Joseph Davis. Unlike other planters who repossessed their lands, Davis sold his acreage to Montgomery, the leader of the Negro community, under very favorable terms. Davis died in 1870, and although he had left a will asking his relatives to "extend a liberal indulgence" concerning Montgomery's payments, Montgomery's land reverted to the Davis family not long after he had taken the Centennial cotton award.[25]

Clearly the Negro, even more so than women and Indians, was the invisible American. When Frederick Douglass, the most famous of all American people of color, arrived on the opening day of the Exposition with a ticket to sit among the dignitaries on the main platform, he was refused admittance. Only when Sen. Roscoe Conkling vouched for his right to be present did he make it to the platform, and although a magnificent orator, he was not asked to address the crowd.

Despite it all, Negroes did go to the Exposition, though no record exists of the exact number. Several publications make mention of their presence. A writer for the *Atlantic Monthly* marveled at the number of stylishly dressed Negroes as well as how many parties consisted of both colored and white people, prompting his hope that "perhaps this new association of colors may mark yet another prejudice conquered."[26] The *Philadelphia Inquirer* had a story on September 27 about a white man attacking a colored man because the latter refused to do the former's bidding. On October 3, the paper carried a story of an unprovoked assault on a Negro by two white men. Letters and family lore provide other evidence of Negro attendance. The existence of a canceled roundtrip train ticket from Washington to Cape May, New Jersey, through Philadelphia in James Wormley's papers indicates his probable presence at the exposition. James E. Waugh, a real estate lawyer, had invited the hotelier to a "Centennial and Cape May Excursion" on August 21. "Trust you will not disappoint me—in fact, you must go."[27] That the ticket was used presupposes Wormley saw the exposition, yet only circumstantial evidence points to this conclusion.

James Wormley had close ties to Philadelphia. His brother William had sent their sister Mary to a Quaker school there; he had belonged to a Negro freemasonry lodge (Laurel Lodge No. 2) in Philadelphia since 1823; when an angry mob came after him for being the Washington agent of William Lloyd Garrison's *Liberator* in 1835, he and John F. Cook, whose son was a close friend of James's, escaped with their lives to Philadelphia; and William had been an officer of the Washington chapter of the Philadelphia Negro Convention Movement. James Wormley's ties to Philadelphia went even deeper. As vice president of the Educational Monument Association, an association founded in 1865 "for the purpose of erecting a Colored People's National Monument to [Lincoln's] memory, . . . a seat of learning . . . for the education of Freemen and Freedmen, and their descendants to be called the National Lincoln Monument Institute," he worked and kept in close touch with Philadelphian Stephen Smith, treasurer of the group. Moreover, the presence of four terrapin restaurants on the fairgrounds—Wissachickon Hall, Maple Spring Hotel, Proskavers, and the Rock Fish Inn—might have enticed Wormley to compare Philadelphia terrapin with his own signature dish. And finally, is it coincidental that Wormley installed the District of Columbia's thirteenth phone in his hotel as soon as possible after the exposition? It seems likely that he had visited Alexander Graham Bell's telephone exhibit in the Education Building.

For all Americans, white as well as colored, Indian and women, the Centennial Exposition, at the very least, offered all people an escape from the endless stories of political corruption in Washington, the collapse of financial and mercantile businesses, and the continuing economic depression that put millions of people out of work. The fair, in fact, was a deliberate response to these conditions in its twin goals of restoring confidence and teaching a lesson about progress, and on this score, it succeeded admirably. The Centennial changed America's image in the world. The official reports of foreign observers were unanimous in their appreciation for the American productive genius. French, British, Swiss, and German observers urged their countrymen to imitate American industry, which had increased the quantity and quality of products through the use of machinery. Before 1876 Europe had looked on the United States as an upstart country; after, as a land of material progress and the world's biggest industrial and economic power. The

Centennial also boosted self-confidence at home. The best news about the Centennial was surely that a multimillion-dollar enterprise had been honestly managed during a time of widespread dishonesty.

Yet all the rhetoric celebrating the country's technology, industrial might, and rising place among the world's leading nations, and all the talk focusing on national unity, fundamentally celebrated a Eurocentric narrative of American history. Exhibits portraying the colonial period, for example, displayed Christopher Columbus, Pilgrims, and Puritans juxtaposed against the savagery of the Indian; portraits and sculptures of Lafayette, Washington, Jefferson, and a rendering of "Yankee Doodle Dandy" presented a portrait of the Revolutionary War; pictures of various white patriots depicted the War of 1812; and images relating to the Civil War included Lincoln, Ulysses Grant, William Seward, Charles Sumner, Robert E. Lee, and Stonewall Jackson. The only allusion to the Negro turned up in a large painting that mingled emancipation and emigration, implying that the legitimate place for the Negro was elsewhere. Exposition managers promoted their version of history in more subtle ways as well. The very method of organizing the thousands of exhibits, to take one example, drove home a message of a hierarchy of progressive to backward peoples. William Phipps Blake, a commissioner from Connecticut and a lineal descendant of one of the earliest settlers of Massachusetts Bay Colony, organized and classified the exhibits.[28] Displays from around the world were organized in the Main Building according to race. The United States, England, France, and Germany got the best areas. France and colonies representing the Latin races were displayed near the northeast central tower; England and colonies representing the Anglo-Saxon races were displayed near the northwest central tower; the German Empire, Austria, and Hungary, representing the Teutonic races, were displayed near the southwest tower; and the United States, with Mexico and Brazil nearby, was displayed near the southeast tower. China, Japan, and Africa were relegated to separate wings, apart from the dominant powers.[29] The values that directed the exhibits into a coherent whole and laid out a logical route for a fair-goer to follow solidified the implied theme of this hierarchy of progressive nations—European countries and the United States—and regressive peoples—China, Japan, and Africa. "Cut off from the rest of the world by its great wall, and isolated behind her old feeling of distrust and apathy towards the peoples of Europe," as the *Public Record* reported, "the old Empire of China has received but little benefit from western civilization and advancement."[30] What the *Public Record* ignored was China's burgeoning trade in silks, jade, and ivory carvings that made Philadelphia's financiers rich and financed the city's shipping industry. The same assumption, that Christian nations were inventive and Asiatic nations imitative, applied to nearly every non-European nation. Take the Orange Free State as an example. Its exhibits, ignoring native African culture, focused on the natural resources of the African continent. This was not surprising since white Americans felt a kindred spirit with white Afrikaners whose struggle with "warlike" blacks who harassed their settlements seemed to white Americans very similar to the colonists' strife with the Indians.

If American Negroes had not noticed that their short yet tenuous hold on social and political rights was slipping before 1876, then the nation's hundred-year birthday celebration should have made this fact abundantly clear. Negroes remained loyal to the Republican Party, but by the time of the Centennial Exposition the party had turned to matters other than civil rights. Although the GOP was the party that supported the main aims of the Civil War, namely the primacy of Union over states' rights, the economic depression that began in 1873 and the country's increasing focus on white sectional reconciliation diminished the political value of focusing on the rights of the freedmen in the eyes of party leaders. Moreover, the contested election, which put the nation's institutions to one of the severest tests they had ever been called upon to endure, deflected attention from Negro concerns.

RESOLUTION OF ELECTION

*S*ince the Civil War, Republicans had been winning elections by stirring emotions with old battle cries. But while they were "raising the bloody flag," their party was changing. Under two Grant administrations the Republicans had become the party of Northern wealth and big business. In the South, however, it was the party of the property-less and oppressed Negro. Northern Republicans, including Rutherford Hayes, began to look on the crusading policy of the Radical Republicans as a liability. What the party needed, they believed, was to win support among white men in the South, men who did all they could to undermine the primacy of the Union, but at the same time, men who shared similar economic views with wealthy Northerners. This was the way to build future party strength as well as to succeed in the immediate goal of taking the presidency. Accordingly, very soon after the election, Hayes's friends got together to plan for both objectives.

One of these friends, William Henry Smith, was general agent of the Western Associated Press, an association of leading newspapers that stretched from New Orleans to Chicago. Smith got other WAP men, like Murat Halstead, proprietor of the *Cincinnati Commercial* and president of the Association; Joseph Medill of the *Chicago Tribune*; Andrew Kellar, editor of the *Memphis Avalanche*; Henry Van Ness Boynton, Washington correspondent for the *Cincinnati Gazette* and later the *Chicago Tribune*; and other like-minded editors to arrange meetings in Washington to assure conservative Democrats of Hayes's good intentions toward the South.

Far more, though, was at stake than the future viability of the Republican Party in the South, or even the future occupant of the White House. What was really at stake in the new year of 1877 was whether the United States could ever again settle a presidential election without resorting to force. Since 1860, when the South seceded rather than accept Lincoln and his strong union ideas, every election—1864, 1868, 1872, and 1876—had turned on the threat and use of military force. Reliance on force as a means of settling political problems had become a habit. To change this practice, it was crucial that the Senate and House committees, chosen just before Congress's Christmas recess, find a workable and peaceful solution to the presidential conundrum.

In Columbus, Ohio, 1877 arrived with a heavy snowfall of almost ten inches. During the day Gov. Rutherford Hayes went sleighing with his children, except for Birch Hayes, who had stayed in Cambridge during his Christmas break from Harvard Law School. Lucy Hayes played hostess to the traditional New Year's Day open house, and probably owing to the suspense over her and her husband's future, 216 friends and neighbors paid their respects.[1]

In Albany, New York, outgoing governor Samuel Tilden escorted his successor, Lucius Robinson, into the Assembly Chamber of the state capitol to take the oath of office. Tilden addressed the chamber, his first public speech since the presidential election. With too much tact and too little passion, the disputed president-elect hopeful reminded his listeners that three years ago Congress had declared the present government of Louisiana illegal, yet its returning board had just reversed the state's popular vote. Making electoral matters worse, Tilden declared the boards in Florida and South Carolina illegal as well. As long as he had used this odd venue and occasion to vent his frustration, he might have mentioned the two congressional committees whose herculean task it was to create a solution to the multiple sets of electoral votes sent to Washington from these very states, but he did not, probably because he believed a solution to any deadlock must come from the House of Representatives, as the Constitution decreed. In fact, to make this point, he wrote the new governor's inaugural address, which Robinson dutifully delivered.

Louisianans welcomed the new year with a dual legislature: Republicans took their seats in the State House while Democrats occupied St. Patrick's Hall. A week later carpetbagger Stephen Packard was sworn in as the Republican governor, and former Confederate brigadier general Francis Nicholls, who had lost an arm and a leg during the war, was inaugurated the Democratic governor. Louisianans were not unduly excited, as the coexistence of dual governors and legislatures was nothing new to them, but in Washington President Grant was not so calm. On Sunday, January 7, the president summoned the cabinet to the White House to deal with the situation.

"It's the Louisiana trouble again," Grant announced. "They are always in trouble there and always wanting the United States to send troops."[2] Since New Year's Day former governor Kellogg had twice telegraphed for additional troops to supplement the small force already protecting the state house. Grant let it be known that he was weary of the use of federal bayonets in deciding elections in the South, so he refused additional troops, at least "until there is actual resistance or conflict."[3]

Telegrams from Louisiana continued to arrive, and Grant kept meeting with the cabinet, which supported sending more troops. In exasperation, the president asked Secretary of State Fish to meet with him on January 17 to explain why he did not want to send more soldiers. Most Americans knew that the returning board had changed a majority of Tilden electors into a majority of Hayes electors, the president said, so it was embarrassing for the Republican Party to defend the status quo. For that reason, he added, he did not wish to meet with the cabinet to discuss this situation, "for I believed there would be six members against me" and, alluding to Fish, "one for me."[4] South Carolina also greeted the New Year with a dual legislature and a dual chief executive. The Republican Daniel Chamberlain was formally inaugurated January 7 and the Democrat, Wade Hampton, on January 14. Both claimed to be the legal authority of the state. The presence of federal troops kept a tense and tenuous peace.

In Florida the New Year brought an end to Reconstruction. All during December the state's courts debated the gubernatorial election. Attorneys for the Democratic candidate, George Drew, obtained an injunction from a circuit judge forbidding the canvassing board to count returns except by merely totaling the votes shown on the county returns with no alterations, a procedure that resulted in a Drew victory. The Republican majority on the canvassing board ignored the injunction and on December 8 announced a win for Republican Marcellus Stearns. The circuit judge cited the board for contempt, ordered a hearing, and applied to the Supreme Court for a writ of mandamus ordering the count. The writ of mandamus was issued by unanimous decision on December 14. The count was made and announced on December 27. Having been careful to avoid any reference to the presidential electors, which might bring the federal courts into the affair, Democrats inaugurated George Drew and a Democratic legislature on January 2.

Former governor Stearns did not protest. The election of Drew, who had been defeated initially by the same count that defeated Tilden, seemed to call into question a Hayes victory, and plenty of Floridians said so. Yet when the last federal troops left Tallahassee on January 18, all such questioning ceased. Florida's fate left only two "unredeemed" Southern states, Louisiana and South Carolina, whose future would be determined by the federal legislature.

Congress went to work January 3. The members of the House committee gathered in the Banking and Currency Committee room, remembered as the room in which John Quincy Adams had died. The Senate's committee deliberated on the opposite side of the Capitol. While both committees caucused, consulted, and cajoled, petitions from businessmen poured into Congress to hurry. "It is impossible to estimate the material loss that the country daily sustains from the existing state of uncertainty," Indiana senator Oliver P. Morton said. "It directly and powerfully tends to unsettle and paralyze business, to weaken public and private credit, and . . . to create doubts of the success of our former government and the perpetuity of the republic."[5] The press, too, urged a speedy settlement, and even the pulpit pleaded for decisiveness.

The first joint meeting of the committees took place on Friday, January 12, in the Senate Judiciary room and continued all through that day and the next. By nightfall two plans for an Electoral Commission had been drawn up, but the group adjourned without final action. The committees met together again on January 15 and 16 and finally agreed on a fifteen-man commission consisting of three Republicans and two Democrats to be elected from the Senate, three Democrats and two Republicans from the House, and four justices of the Supreme Court, two Democrats and two Republicans, who together would choose a fifth justice, whom everyone assumed would be David Davis, a Lincoln campaign manager and appointee to the Court and the only avowed Independent, thereby constituting a commission with seven Republicans, seven Democrats, and one Independent.

Neither Hayes nor Tilden liked this plan. Hayes wanted the president of the Senate, Republican Thomas Ferry, to count the vote, and Tilden would have liked to stand fast on what he called "the Constitution and the settled practice of counting votes," namely, that the House should determine the next president.

The Electoral Commission Bill the joint committees had drawn up went to the Senate; it passed on January 25. As the House voted and passed the bill on January 26, word that Justice Davis had won a surprise election to the Senate by the Illinois legislature in a Democratic-Greenback coalition reached the House. The news greatly disturbed Democratic National Committee chairman Abram Hewitt. "I [had] taken pains to investigate Judge Davis thoroughly, and the best information I [got was] that he is neutral."[6]

Davis had not been a candidate or even an aspirant to the Senate, but the Illinois legislature, evenly divided between Republicans and Democrats, had been trying since January 17 to elect a senator. On the fortieth ballot, the Independents joined the Democrats and chose David Davis. As his close friend and one-time secretary wrote, he was thrilled. He had wanted off the Supreme Court for a long time, having grown "weary of the conflicting and monotonous work of the court." And what's more, he "sternly objected to the invention of an Electoral Commission to make a president after the people had voted and elected one," and he "was unwilling to assume a responsibility, however honestly it might be exercised, [that] would subject him to misrepresentation in history, by the defeated party."[7]

Democrats faced a range of choices for the fifth judge that had narrowed to out-and-out Republicans. They finally acquiesced in the selection of Joseph Bradley of New Jersey as the fifth justice after assurance of his neutrality. Bradley, a Grant Republican, was the person who bore principal responsibility for the invalidation of key provisions of the Enforcement Act of 1870 and the Fourteenth and Fifteenth Amendments in the Slaughterhouse, Cruikshank, and Reese cases. Hewitt was suspicious of Bradley's supposed neutrality. The Electoral Commission now had eight Republicans and seven Democrats who would choose the next president of the United States. On January 29, Grant signed the bill into law.

While deliberations of the congressional committees separately and jointly slowly moved forward during January, Samuel Tilden, with the help of John Bigelow and Manton Marble, continued working on compiling a history of the electoral counts from the George Washington presidential election through the current one that they had begun in December. When it was finished at the end of January, they published the result under the title *Presidential Counts*. This exercise in futility was quintessential Tilden. Not understanding that as head of a party at a time of extreme crisis he should have assigned the task to an underling, he put all his energy in showing conclusively that Ferry could not rightfully count the electoral votes. All precedents made this clear. In the past votes had been routinely counted by a group of three tellers, one from the Senate and two from the House. Occasions did occur when the tellers disagreed, but since the presidency did not depend on the count, a decision had been evaded by counting votes in both ways.

While Tilden wasted away valuable time in an exercise of little value, Hayes stayed in communication with his Western Associated Press friends who, during December, had been meeting with and trying to win Southern Democrats to the Republican side. There is no evidence, however, that these early meetings continued into January or even into the first half of February. While Tilden still had a chance to become the official president elect through the decision of the Electoral Commission, Southerners bided their time. James Garfield, a member of the Electoral Commission and a fellow Ohioan in close touch with Hayes, recorded no visits of Southern congressmen in his diary, nor did letters from the WAP people to Hayes make any mention of meetings with white Southerners. What these letters did tell, however, was their supposition of what Southerners wanted more than they wanted the presidency, namely a chance to share in the federal largesse that had gone to Northern business interests, especially railroads. Since Tilden had campaigned on ending the free-and-easy subsidies and public handouts of the Grant administration, might not that alone be enough to impel at least some Southerners to jump ship?

Accordingly, the WAP coalition dangled the bait of a Southern railroad, specifically a railroad through Texas to California. The Union-Pacific/Central Pacific Railroad, built with lavish federal assistance when Southern senators and representatives were absent from Congress, had become a reality. As Hayes's friends well knew, the ambition for a competing line through Texas was very much alive. To these men, a peaceful solution to the crisis, Hayes's inauguration, and strong Republican inroads in the South all hinged on Republican assurances of internal improvement subsidies, primarily subsidies for the Texas and Pacific Railroad. Thomas A. Scott, vice president of the sprawling Pennsylvania Railroad, had actually secured from Congress in 1872 a land grant of almost sixteen million acres for a railroad that would run from Marshall, Texas, through El Paso to San Diego. A paltry two hundred miles of track had been laid when the Wall Street panic hit the entire country in 1873 and work stopped. To encourage federal assistance in the form of cash, Scott agreed to add parallel branch lines connecting the Texas road to St. Louis, Memphis, Vicksburg, Baton Rouge, and New Orleans, all calculated to make the Texas and Pacific irresistible to congressional representatives of that region. Despite much back-and-forth lobbying, the railroad deal just was not enough of an issue around which to engineer the political realignment of the

South,[8] but the backroom maneuvering had been so widespread that newspapers started publishing stories about the embryonic deal. "There is undoubtedly danger of defection among Southern Democrats," the *New York Sun* reported.[9] Montgomery Blair, who ran the Democratic paper, the D.C. *Union*, complained to Tilden that "the railroad men in Congress have sold you out."[10] As it turned out Scott was never able to get his scheme off the floor of the House for a vote.[11] At the time it was known that more than half, forty out of seventy-three Southern representatives, would have opposed it.[12]

As the Electoral Commission determined its organization, rules, and meeting place on the last two days of January, the five lawyers chosen to represent the Republicans and the six acting for Tilden checked into various hotels and settled in for a stay of at least five weeks. Business for James Wormley was especially brisk, because the two lead Republican lawyers, William Evarts and Stanley Matthews, chose to stay at Wormley's hotel. Even before the Electoral Commission began its serious business, Wormley's became the principal focal point for Republican strategizing as well as socializing.

On Thursday, February 1, the House and Senate met in joint session at one p.m. in the Hall of the House of Representatives, and Thomas Ferry, as presiding officer, called the joint meeting of the two branches of Congress to begin the electoral count as prescribed by statute.[13] As agreed, when there was only one return, the vote would be counted. When there was more than one return, the matter went directly to the Electoral Commission. Senator Ferry picked up the certificate from Alabama, the first state in an alphabetical list of states, opened it, and passed it to the tellers, one of whom announced the vote—ten votes for Tilden—and so the count continued until Florida. With three sets of votes from that state, the conflicting certificates and all relevant papers went to the Electoral Commission for the decision as to which was the "true and lawful electoral vote of the state."[14]

The Electoral Commission met in the room of the Supreme Court on February 2. The fifteen commissioners sat around a rectangular table. For five days the commission listened to arguments from the lawyers—one lawyer for the Democrats, David Dudley Field, was the brother of Democratic Commissioner Justice Stephen Field—and then for two days, after all spectators and counsel vacated the room, considered the question behind closed doors. The crux of the case, over which debate lasted for almost a week, was whether the commission would go "behind" the formal certificates and inquire into the validity of the state electoral canvass itself. There was precedent for congressional scrutiny and rejection of suspect electoral votes as recently as in 1872 in the cases of Louisiana and Arkansas.[15] On February 8 the commissioners resumed public hearings and on February 10 announced their decision. By a vote along party lines of 8-7 they gave Florida's electoral votes to Hayes. Hayes jubilantly recorded in his diary, "It shows the strength of party ties."[16] On Monday, February 12, the House voted 168-103 (19 abstaining) to reject the decision. Since the Senate had accepted the decision and since the act creating the Electoral Commission provided that its decision should be final unless both branches of Congress acted separately, the House rejection did not matter.

The count continued until Louisiana was reached. Again the Democrats sought to go behind the returns and bring proof of the frauds that created a majority for the Hayes electors. Again the Republicans stood squarely on the certificate of the canvassing board on the principle of the right of a state to adhere to its own election laws without federal interference. And again the commission voted, eight for accepting the Hayes electors and seven for accepting Tilden's. When the Louisiana vote was submitted to the Senate for its ratification, the Republicans all but admitted canvassing board frauds. "Mr. President," John Sherman said, "a good deal is said about fraud, fraud, fraud—fraud and perjury, and wrong. Why, Sir, if you go behind the returns in Louisiana, the case is stronger for the Republicans than upon the face of the returns. What do you find there? Crime, murder, violence, that is what you find. . . . I say now, as I said two months ago that while there may have been irregularities, while there may have been a non-observance of some directory laws, yet the substantial right was arrived at by the action of the returning board."[17] Again, the House of Representatives rejected the decision, but as the Senate accepted it, on February, 16 the vote of Louisiana was counted for Hayes.

At this vote, Maj. Edward A. Burke, who had managed Nicholls's gubernatorial campaign and who had been sent to Washington as Nicholls's personal representative to obtain a commitment from Hayes and his friends that governors Nicholls and Hampton would remain in power after a Hayes inauguration, let it be known that he was ready to talk to Republican leaders. "My people expected me to do all that I could to secure Mr. Tilden in his rightful possession, and I felt unwilling to hold any consultation . . . so long as there was hope or prospect of seating Mr. Tilden," Burke said. "When that hope passed away (on the 16 of February), we were then ready to discuss the subject [home rule] with Mr. Hayes's friends."[18]

Burke spoke to several of Hayes's allies, describing the volatile state of affairs in New Orleans owing to their fear that Governor Packard would survive and not

Nicholls. Everyone Burke talked to insisted that no one in Washington wanted the continuation of carpetbag rule. Still, as Burke told Stanley Matthews, a Hayes adviser and one of the Republican lawyers for the Hayes electors, he felt assured about Hayes's attitude toward Louisiana but questioned the good will of men like John Sherman and James Garfield. He doubted that Hayes could implement any change of policy against their opposition. Matthews said he could not speak for them. In that case, Burke replied, the congressmen from Louisiana would lead a filibuster in the House in order to prevent the electoral count from being completed in time for Hayes to be inaugurated on March 4.

Burke was bluffing. The Democratic caucus had just voted not to impede the count of the electoral vote, and Burke knew this. He might not have gotten away with this deception had it not been for a journalistic accident. "Why Don't the Republican Majority Govern Louisiana," screamed the headline of a long editorial in the February 22 *Ohio State Journal*.[19] A somewhat standard bloody shirt diatribe, it urged the president to recognize Governor Packard immediately and sustain him by the use of troops. The editorial occasioned unusual attention because the editor of the *Ohio State Journal*, Gen. James Comly, was well known in Washington as one of Governor Hayes's closest friends. In fact, General Comly was one of those who had gone to the capital in January with "honeyed" words of the new Republican policy toward the South.

The morning after the article had appeared in Columbus, fifty marked copies were circulated among Democratic members in the House. They created a sensation, since it was assumed the editorial represented Hayes's view of Louisiana. Later it was learned that Comly had been sick, that the article had been written by a young man at the newspaper, and that Hayes had known nothing about it. But the article gave Major Burke just what he needed. The threat of a filibuster seemed real, giving Burke the opportunity to pressure Republicans.

Meanwhile, the count continued until Oregon, a state with two sets of returns that were sent to the commission. The Democratic counsel took the position that if the commission followed its own precedents, they must find that the certificate with the electoral vote for Tilden, the one properly certified by the governor, was the lawful certificate. In other words, the Democrats now espoused the Republican argument that neither Congress nor the commission had the right to go behind the governor's certificate. If logic meant anything, the Democratic return was in the same class as the accepted returns for Florida and Louisiana. But, since the loss of even one challenged elector, who had held a federal job and thus was constitutionally ineligible to serve as an elector, would give the presidency to Tilden, the Republican lawyers squelched the Democrats' position. Evarts, as lead lawyer, argued that there was a radical distinction between the Southern states and Oregon. To go behind the returns in the South would require a recount of the whole popular vote, a scrutiny of innumerable questions of intimidation and fraud, and a broad substitution of federal for state authority, whereas the Oregon case involved a mere correction of the governor's action. Casting illogic aside, the commissioners, voting along party lines as always, awarded Oregon's electors to Hayes.

On Monday morning, February 23, after the Oregon vote, Major Burke met with President Grant. After, he telegraphed Nicholls that the president "says unequivocally that he is satisfied that the Nicholls government is the government which should stand in Louisiana, and that he believes it will stand, because it is sustained by the most influential elements of the state, and that the Packard government cannot exist without the support of troops."[20]

Shortly after meeting Grant, Burke went to see Senator Sherman, who had just agreed to serve in Hayes's cabinet as secretary of the treasury. Sherman asked what it would take to stop the filibuster. Burke showed the senator the wire he had just sent Nicholls. Sherman assured Burke that Hayes would pursue the same plan as Grant.

While Burke choreographed an agreement among Republican leaders to keep Nicholls in office, the votes of South Carolina came up for consideration before the commission. As a last resort, the Democrats changed their legal strategy.[21] They asked that the votes of South Carolina not be counted, arguing that there had been no provision made for the registration of persons entitled to vote, that the presence of federal troops at or near polling places was unconstitutional, and that there was not a democratic form of government in South Carolina. Because of these circumstances, Tilden lawyers argued, there had been no legal election. The commission, not surprisingly, decided by a strict party vote to award South Carolina's electoral votes to Hayes.

The Republicans won the votes of all three of the contested Southern states plus Oregon not only because they had one more commissioner than the Democrats—and all votes were 8-7 for Hayes electors—but also because William Evarts orchestrated their judicial tactics in all cases and even argued his position before the commission in the Florida, Louisiana, Oregon, and South Carolina disputes. His commanding presence, even in strategy sessions at Wormley's, accounts for the unity and consistency of the Republican claim. He even had a hand, at least indirectly, in the behind-the-scenes finagling referred to as the Wormley Bargain because it was in his quarters at the hotel on the night of February 26 that Burke and Louisiana members of the House, E. John Ellis and William Levy, met with five Ohioans, commission lawyer Stanley Matthews, former governor William Dennison, Charles Foster (member of the House of Representatives from Hayes's own Cincinnati district and the only Ohio member who supported the Electoral Commission Bill),[22] John Sherman, and James Garfield, all close Hayes associates.[23] Henry Watterson, the nephew of Stanley Matthews, also attended, charged with overseeing South Carolina's concerns.

As a member of the still-in-progress Electoral Commission, Garfield felt uncomfortable being present at the meeting. Later that night he wrote in his diary that he left the meeting early because what he said so displeased Stanley Matthews. All he said was what others had been saying, namely that he "had no doubt that the new administration would deal justly and generously with the South, and the whole nation would honor those southern men who are resisting anarchy, and thus are preventing civil war."[24] What annoyed Matthews, no doubt, was his statement that those meeting together in Evarts's room could not "afford to do anything that would appear to be a political bargain."[25]

"There was no bargain, there was no talk of bargain," John Ellis insisted. "The only matter that transpired on that evening was an interchange of views eliciting on our part from these chosen, well-recognized, close friends of Mr. Hayes his views with regard to [Louisiana and South Carolina]. These gentlemen pledged nothing for Mr. Hayes; they bound him to no promise."[26] The day after the Wormley meeting, E. A. Burke talked on the record with the Associated Press, saying that "the original parties were bound not to divulge anything concerning the arrangement except for violated faith, which has not occurred," a statement that certainly undercut Ellis's assertion.[27]

Ellis had gone to the meeting specifically to question Stanley Matthews. Representative Lamar from Mississippi had told Ellis that Matthews had insisted that it would be Hayes's policy to have "nothing to do with Packard and Chamberlain, nor with the carpetbag governments in those two states."[28] So when Ellis met Matthews at Wormley's, he got right to the heart of his concern. "I don't exactly see how Governor Nicholls and Governor Hampton are going to succeed in Louisiana and South Carolina as the governors of those states. For instance, the party and the people who have supported Mr. Hayes have supported Mr. Packard; they have run together at the polls, and I do not see how Mr. Hayes is going to be awarded the electoral vote of Louisiana, Mr. Packard ousted, and Mr. Nicholls put in, nor how the same result can be attained in South Carolina."[29] Matthews said he saw no problem as the president would pursue a policy of noninterference.

In return for nonintervention the Louisianans pledged to protect the civil and political rights of Negroes and to promote equal educational opportunity. They also broached the matter of Louisiana's senate seats. The term of J. R. West was about to expire. The Republican legislature had already elected William Kellogg, the former governor. The other seat had been vacant since the disputed election of 1872, the Senate having repeatedly denied Pinckney Benton Stewart Pinchback, the Republican claimant, the right to assume office. The state's Democratic legislature had recently chosen James B. Eustis to fill the remaining two years of this "short term." Worried about the control of the next Senate, the Ohioans got Burke, Levy, and Ellis to promise that the Nicholls legislature would postpone the election of a rival for Kellogg's seat until after March 10.[30] By that time, they reasoned, Kellogg would probably have been sworn in by the Senate.

Despite assurances given and agreements made at Wormley's, serious unease among Southern Democrats in the House kept the filibuster idea alive. Abram Hewitt, resigned to Tilden's loss and desirous of a peaceful end to what still could be an explosive situation, namely no president-elect by March 4, deliberately delayed the count for one day. Gen. Richard Taylor, the only son of former president Zachary Taylor and a Louisiana resident, had been his houseguest throughout the entire electoral crisis, and through Taylor, Hewitt kept abreast of negotiations between Burke and the Hayes people.

"I hold in my hand," Hewitt said on Wednesday, February 28, on the floor of the House when the count had reached Vermont, "a package which purports to contain electoral votes from the state of Vermont. This package was delivered to me by express about the middle of December last, and a similar package had been forwarded by mail to the presiding officer of the Senate." Hewitt offered Senator Thomas Ferry the package, "the seals of which are unbroken and which is how as it came into my possession."[31]

Senator Ferry refused to accept the results contained in packet, for it declared that a Democratic candidate for elector had been chosen because one of the Republican candidates was a postmaster. The joint session adjourned for the day with no action. After adjournment, Burke once again got an interview with Grant, who promised the Louisianan he would order the withdrawal of troops as soon as the electoral count was completed. Hewitt, through Taylor, was privy to this information.[32]

The next day, Thursday, March 1, three days from the end of Grant's presidency, the galleries and halls of the House were jammed with spectators to watch the proceedings. Nearly the entire Senate came to do likewise. After two hours of debate, a by-now-convinced Representative Levy stood to announce his intention of throwing no obstacle (filibuster) "in the way of the completion of the electoral count," and he called upon "those of my fellow-members who have been influenced in their action upon this question by a desire to protect Louisiana and South Carolina to join me in the course which I feel called upon and justified in pursuing."[33]

At this signal to continue the count, the House voted 148-116 to place Vermont's electors in the Hayes column. The Senate then joined the House on the floor and the joint count resumed. Virginia and West Virginia posed no problems, but new objections greeted the Wisconsin count.

Tilden diehards made one last attempt to save the presidency. The Senate retired to its chamber while the House debated whether to accept Wisconsin's returns. At this critical moment a telegram from Tilden arrived that appealed to all Democrats to let the vote be concluded. Speaker of the House Randall sent a messenger to the Senate that the House was ready to receive it. The vote was completed at four a.m. Friday, March 2. Members had been in session for eighteen consecutive hours. In dazed exhaustion Ferry said, "Whereupon I do declare that Rutherford B. Hayes, having received a majority of the whole number of electoral votes [185-184], is duly elected President of the United States for four years, commencing on the 4th of March, 1877." And so John Ellis's prediction that the Electoral Commission, which he had reluctantly voted for, would turn out to be a "mere national returning board" had come true.[34]

Hayes had resigned as governor two days earlier and at the time Ferry announced his election, he was fast asleep in a private railroad car furnished by Tom Scott of the Pennsylvania Railroad. About dawn Friday, March 2, he was awakened as the train neared Harrisburg and told that he was officially president-elect. Two thousand people met his train in Washington despite heavy rain. The Sherman brothers, Senator John, and army commander William Tecumseh, escorted him to a waiting carriage and to John Sherman's home. On March 3, President and Mrs. Grant entertained the Hayes family at dinner at the White House. Because March 4 fell on a Sunday, to avoid an interregnum, Grant asked Chief Justice Morrison Waite to administer the oath of office privately to Hayes in the Red Room. On a cold Monday, March 5, at noon Hayes repeated his oath and delivered his address before 30,000 people. Because of the long and bitter election dispute there was no inaugural parade or ball.

As promised, Grant had sent a telegram to New Orleans instructing General Christoper Augur to withdraw protection from Packard. Whether Grant knew it or not, Secretary of War Donald Cameron stopped the order,[35] and, as if in collaboration, General Sherman told Augur to go slow. So, despite the Grant administration's having ordered the end of military occupation, the final decision was left to Hayes. On March 6 Hayes met with Grant's outgoing cabinet to ask if "any consideration [had] been given the question of a de facto as distinguished from a de jure state government?"[36] Four cabinet members favored recognizing the Packard government. Chandler, as one of them, made the irrefutable point that the Packard government was chosen on the same vote on which Hayes had been declared president.

Hayes dealt with South Carolina first. Stanley Matthews wrote to Chamberlain from Wormley's to ask him to arrange matters in such a way as to obviate the need for troops. Chamberlain was so annoyed by Matthews's request that Hayes invited him and his rival gubernatorial claimant to Washington. Hampton urged the removal of troops and pledged to respect the rights of the freedmen. Hayes brought the matter before his own cabinet, which agreed: the troops must go. Accordingly, Secretary of War George McCrary, the congressman from Iowa who suggested the House and Senate committee that created the Electoral Commission, directed General Augur to withdraw the troops. On April 10, 1877, they marched out of the state house. The next day Chamberlain surrendered his office.

Louisiana was a more embarrassing situation to settle than South Carolina, where Hampton may or may not have been elected. In Louisiana, Packard had received a much larger vote than Hayes and was, in a way, more legitimately elected than the president was. In other words, if Packard was not elected, Hayes had not carried the state. Hayes was now safely inaugurated, and while many millions disputed his right to have been inaugurated, no one had taken up arms against him. Hayes had to let the carpetbagger government down easy, or he would have the wrath of the Republican North upon him. So he appointed a commission, against which William Chandler railed bitterly.

The commission reached New Orleans on April 5. The members of the Packard legislature were invited to join the Nicholls legislature in return for back pay. The offer of money was irresistible. Assistance of another kind came from the Louisiana Lottery Company, which contributed $40,000 to bribe Packard's remaining legislators.[37] The Packard legislature melted away, and by the third week in April all Negro legislators were in the Democratic assembly. On April 24, as the clock atop Saint Louis Cathedral struck the noonday hour, federal troops marched away from the state house and the forsaken Packard fled its grounds. Reconstruction was over. Suddenly, spontaneously, a public celebration began to the cacophony of clanging bells and thundering cannon. The streets of the city looked like Mardi Gras, although far rowdier than the one just past, occurring as it did on a cold, rainy February day. Happy, ecstatic white citizens, finally, after fifteen long years, "redeemed," kept the revelry going the rest of the day and all night. To forestall future restiveness among the ousted, Hayes gave jobs to the forty-seven Negro members of the Louisiana legislature who lost employment when Democrats assumed power in the state, and he made sure that Stephen Packard, the probable winner of the governorship, got awarded the consulship of Liverpool, a position then regarded as the pick of federal posts for its lucrative fees. And to express special gratitude to those who made his presidency possible, he granted federal jobs to all members of the returning board, despite their indictments by a state court, to some of their relatives, and to their secretaries.[38]

Hayes reaped the glory among white Southerners for restoring home rule, but President Grant had already given up "bayonet rule" by reassigning most of the federal forces that held up carpetbag governments even before Hayes assumed office. And anyway, Hayes did not remove troops, but reassigned them from the capitals of Columbia and New Orleans to their previous places of nearby encampment.

Although getting rid of the military was paramount to white Southerners, its presence was not much more than symbolic. The entire army of the United States, including Indian scouts, chaplains, medical personnel, ordnance officers, quartermaster sergeants, and West Point cadets, totaled only 25,000 men at this time, and most of these troops were fighting Indians on the plains or protecting the Mexican and Indian frontier of Texas. Excluding Texas, only 3,230 officers and men were on duty in the South in the spring of 1877. In Louisiana soldiers were scattered in sixty-two locations. Hayes's order to remove the troops did not result in a single soldier's leaving the South. Later in the year many companies were transferred because of railroad strikes and Indian troubles in other parts of the country.[39]

In the 130 years since the February meeting at James Wormley's hotel, the story has been passed down that Republicans as represented by Hayes's associates John

Sherman, Stanley Matthews, William Dennison, James Garfield, and Charles Foster agreed to abandon Republican state governments in Louisiana and South Carolina in return for the willingness of Southern Democrats as represented by E. A. Burke, John Ellis, William Levy, and Henry Watterson, to abandon a filibuster in the House, thereby bargaining away the presidency in return for the end of Reconstruction. While it is true that Hayes became president and the Republican governors and legislatures in Louisiana and South Carolina were abandoned by the national party, and the filibuster in the House was broken, all of this would have happened whether or not there had been a Wormley meeting, agreement, bargain, compromise—by whatever name it is known.

As Henry Watterson, one of the Wormley House participants put it, "Hayes was already as good as seated. If the states of Louisiana and South Carolina could save their local autonomy out of the general wreck, there seemed no good reason to forbid."[40] A leading Southern newspaper correspondent, Lucius Quintus Washington, wrote early in 1877 to rebut "the silly charge of the bargain. Southern congressmen did not give away Mr. Tilden, nor could they do so."[41] The prize, Mr. Washington wrote, was "lost by the inaction and submission, or prudence—call it what you will—of our northern allies. They, not the South or her congressmen, went back on Mr. Tilden." He could have added that while Tilden sat in his Gramercy Park study, drafting interminable, nitpicking constitutional briefs, the Republicans seized the initiative and held it. Moreover, Tilden's defeat was the work of a partisan Electoral Commission, the rigged returning boards, ballot-box stuffers, and bribers. In fact, instead of blaming the electoral crisis for causing the abandonment of Reconstruction, it would be more accurate to argue that the abandonment of Reconstruction caused the crisis of 1876–1877.[42] Had Republicans been willing to intervene in defense of black rights, Tilden would not have won almost the entire South, in which case there would not have been the disputed election. Nor can it be said that Republicans abandoned the Negro to obtain the presidency, for the party, not to mention the Supreme Court, had in large part already abandoned his cause.

Rutherford Hayes himself had determined to change tactics. Despite his encouragement of the bloody shirt rhetoric during the election campaign, Hayes gave many signals that he was changing his mind about the South and Reconstruction. During the years since college, he had kept up with a Texan classmate, Guy M. Bryan, who in letter after letter urged a more moderate policy toward the South and pushed for local self-government. "You will see in my letter of acceptance," Hayes wrote Bryan after winning the Republican nomination, "the influence of the feeling which our friendship has tended to foster."[43]

As early as 1875 during the gubernatorial campaign Hayes called for reconciliation between North and South. Moreover, many Republican leaders supported Hayes's developing let-alone policy; even men like James Blaine and Roscoe Conkling started questioning the desirability of keeping state governments propped up by troops. Businessmen especially deplored the use of federal troops for the simple reason that their presence was bad for business. Marshall Jewell, a favorite son candidate from Connecticut at the '76 Republican convention, told Hayes that businessmen needed stable Southern governments, which would occur if troops left and the "best"—never defined—white men returned to power in the South.

Within two months of taking office Hayes returned home rule to the last of the "unredeemed" states and appointed a Southerner, David McKendree Key, postmaster general, the chief patronage-dispensing office of the cabinet, signaling loudly and clearly his intent to reconcile North and South and a change in Republican policy. While the Republican Party, especially the new president, had definitely not written off the South, it was clear that both the party and president wanted to rejuvenate a Southern Republican party, this time among the very whites who espoused states' rights.

STATES' RIGHTS
RIDE SUPREME

*T*he Republican Party did achieve its goal of converting white Southerners, but
not during the Hayes administration, even despite the unprecedented and
nonstop flow of federal funds that moved south from 1877 to 1880. Southern
Democrats in 1877 introduced forty bills in the Senate and 267 in the House asking for and often getting money for projects in their respective states.[1] Hayes went
out of his way to dispense federal patronage to white conservatives throughout
the South, and in so doing angered its Republicans. He made two trips throughout the South, preaching reconciliation. None of this impelled white Democrats
to switch party allegiance. Nor did Republicans fare any better in the next seventeen administrations. The white South remained solidly Democratic until new
civil rights legislation was signed into law in 1964, nearly a century after Hayes's
presidency, by a Southern Democratic president, which impelled white Southerners
to switch parties en masse, giving Republican presidential candidates the solid
support they once gave Democrats.

Despite widespread fear of a resurgence of Reconstruction in the South, a
bloody yet short-lived strike of railroad workers, four short months after Hayes's
inauguration, signaled loudly and clearly that Republicans had become far more
interested in protecting business than in protecting freedmen's civil rights. On
July 16 workers on the Baltimore and Ohio Railroad walked off their jobs in
Martinsburg, West Virginia, to protest a wage cut. The strike spread along trunk

lines to every part of the country except New England and the Deep South. Workers in other industries organized sympathy strikes. All demanded an eight-hour workday, a return to pre-depression wages, and an end to child labor. Local militias formed to contain the strikers.

Desperate fighting broke out in Chicago. In a single clash between police and "a mob of the dangerous classes" ten rioters were killed and forty-five wounded.[2] In Pittsburgh twenty people died when militiamen fired on crowds that had seized railroad switches. Outraged onlookers set fire to the Pittsburgh railroad yards, destroying a hundred locomotives and two thousand railroad cars. State governors, railroad executives, the president's cabinet (made up chiefly of corporate attorneys and railroad directors), and Thomas A. Scott, the president of the Pennsylvania Railroad who also had direct access to the White House, urged Hayes to send federal troops to quell the strikes. Without any investigation as to need and without setting guidelines as to their use, the president promptly filled all requests for federal troops from Buffalo to St. Louis. Hayes wrote in his diary that he had to call out federal troops to protect "by force" the property of the railroad companies.[3] The soldiers, not surprisingly, did not act as impartial defenders of order; they protected railroad owners by aiding non-striking workers, by opening railroad lines, and by preventing unions from holding meetings. By the end of July the Great Strike had been put down by force. The War Department issued a pamphlet on riot duty and constructed for the first time a system of armories in major cities to house a standing National Guard.

In Europe at the time, former president Grant expressed astonishment at how approving most citizens seemed to be of the use of federal troops to protect property when but a short time before he had been denounced for using them to protect civil rights and lives. "During my two terms of office the whole Democratic press, and the morbidly honest and 'reformatory' portion of the Republican press, thought it horrible to keep U.S. troops stationed in the southern states, and when they were called upon to protect the lives of Negroes . . . the country was scarcely large enough to hold the sound of indignation belched forth by them for some years. Now, however, there is no hesitation about exhausting the whole power of government to suppress a strike on the slightest intimation that danger threatens."[4] The handling of the Great Strike showed how devoted Republican Party leaders had become to the protection and preservation of vested interests rather than upholding the idea of a powerful national state protecting fundamental rights of all American citizens. The cause of the Negro suffered as a result.

When Hayes thought he had lost the '76 election, he wrote in his diary that he did not mind defeat but worried about "the poor colored men of the South." When he did become president, he never took the initiative in prodding Congress to take action to protect Negroes. Still, he did oppose all efforts to weaken existing federal legislation. When Democrats, who had a slight majority in both houses, passed a rider to the army appropriation bill barring the use of troops to keep peace at the polls, Hayes vetoed the law on April 29, 1879. In all, during his four-year presidency, he vetoed eight bills designed to weaken federal protection of the rights of Negroes.[5] And in all his messages to Congress he called attention to the violation of the constitutional rights of Negroes. But however well-intentioned Hayes may have been toward the "poor colored men of the South," his real priority had been to bring white Southerners into the Republican fold and effect a reconciliation between the North and South.

Midway into Hayes's presidency, the matter of who was to run the District of Columbia was finally settled. The Act of 1878 stipulated that Congress would govern the federal area with three presidentially approved commissioners serving as executives, and, in return for the denial of any local say about taxes and other local problems, the federal government would share expenses equally with District taxpayers. The commissioners would appoint the police, a school board, and a health officer. The president would also name the justices of the District Supreme Court. Negroes had made greater strides in Washington than anywhere else in the United States, but this act, which abruptly disenfranchised native Washingtonians, ended political associations between Negroes and whites. A well-established family like the Wormleys at first felt none of these changes, but they were well aware of what this trend portended for the future.

However disappointed, even worried, James Wormley might have been by recent developments, he worked as hard and as productively as before. When people marveled at his extraordinary achievement, he always said, "I owe my success to the prompt payment of those I employ and the settlement of my bills as they are presented."[6] Clearly his renown was based on more than a prompt discharge of bills; although his strict punctuality and integrity were part of it, his superb accommodations, refined cuisine, perfect service, his affability, and always making a point of personally welcoming arriving guests and thanking them when they left—all account for Wormley's being looked on as the model hotel of the capital and the hotel preferred over any other Washington establishment by European travelers. Several legations set up housekeeping at the hotel in the 1870s and

1880s, including the German, French, and Chilean delegations. A large part of any Foreign Service officer's job was entertaining, and in this Wormley's excelled. The Spanish minister who lived at the hotel, for example, gave an annual ball well known for its floral extravagance. Each year Wormley's workers transformed the hotel's first floor into an arboretum. The long parlors were enveloped with orange trees, magnolias, and banks of flowers that completely covered several of the doors. "Even the chandeliers were a mass of flowers," wrote twenty-year-old Lizzie Sherman, niece of John Sherman, to her mother in Cleveland about the 1877 ball.[7]

A short time after the party Henry Adams and his wife, Clover, moved to Washington and became neighbors of Wormley's Hotel when they set up house-keeping in William Corcoran's "yellow house" at 1501 H Street. Because Adams boarded his horse at Wormley's stables in Tenleytown, he saw quite a lot of James Wormley and, like so many other neighbors of the hotel, came to depend on him for household matters. Most important to Adams was Wormley's expert handling of arrangements to ship the horse to the Adamses' summer home at Beverly Farms, Massachusetts. "I have been riding him this afternoon and he seems no worse for the journey," Adams wrote the hotelier in 1878. "I am so sorry to have given you so much trouble, but am really very much obliged, for I know of no one whom I would ask to help me but yourself, and we were anxious about the horse."[8]

In November of the following year electric lights came to Washington for the first time when a statue of Gen. George H. Thomas, a Virginian who had re-mained loyal to the Union, was unveiled at Thomas Circle and lighted with power brought to Fourteenth Street and Massachusetts Avenue from a Thirteenth Street sawmill. As soon afterward as he was able, Wormley installed electric lights at the hotel, a marvel Henry and Clover Adams enjoyed when they moved in for a few months at the end of 1880. After an extended trip to Europe, the Adamses took a six-year lease on another of William Corcoran's houses, this one at 1607 H Street, facing Lafayette Square. While the couple remodeled the six-bedroom townhouse complete with stable—no more horse boarding at Tenleytown—with a five-room annex for servants' quarters above, they lived at the hotel. Their monthly hotel bill was roughly the equivalent of their monthly rent in the Corcoran house—$200.

By the time Clover and Henry Adams had moved out of the hotel and into the house on H Street, Wormley had undertaken a major renovation of the hotel that included adding rooms. In the midst of the renovation, on May 24, 1881, Wormley received notice that Patent #242091 was his. Years before, he had applied for a patent for a life-saving apparatus for boats that he had invented.

Only weeks later, as Wormley's renovation continued, a crazed gunman seriously wounded President James Garfield. On the morning of July 2, 1881, four months after his inauguration, a disappointed office seeker shot him in the back as the president strolled arm in arm with Secretary of State Blaine across the waiting room of the Baltimore and Potomac Railroad Station not far from the hotel. During Garfield's convalescence in the White House, Wormley prepared special foods for the president, and even when he was transferred by special train, at his own request, to Elberon, New Jersey, Wormley sent instructions and implements for the preparation of these same foods. Not that Garfield's doctors let him eat any of Wormley's food. Confined to a milk and chicken broth diet, later expanded to include oatmeal and limewater, the president grew weaker while his doctors probed his body trying in vain to locate the bullet.[9] By late August, after two failed operations, one without ether, Garfield's body had shrunk to 130 pounds, half its normal weight. He was literally starving to death as those taking care of him enjoyed Wormley's food. Even during his last two weeks of life, spent in a bed in a cottage owned by a New York financier in Elberon, Wormley's food kept arriving, but by this time Garfield had no strength to ask for a taste of it. He died there on September 9.

Garfield's assassination, perpetrated as it was by a disgruntled individual who sought a diplomatic post as his reward for having supported the president's election, aroused national sentiment to fix the civil service. Reformers had been calling for an end to the spoils system for more than a decade, but nothing came of their attempts until Democratic senator George Pendleton of Ohio proposed a bill in 1882 that would create a bipartisan three-man Civil Service Commission to oversee a merit system for hiring federal bureaucrats. When the bill passed, proponents worried whether President Chester Arthur would veto it. After all, as the collector of the New York Customhouse, he had been a longtime and big-time beneficiary of the spoils system. He signed the Pendleton Act in 1883, angering old friends, especially Sen. Roscoe Conkling, and delighting former critics, and appointed three men well known as advocates of civil service reform, notably its chairman, Dorman B. Eaton, a leader of the reform movement in New York and author of the Pendleton Act. The new law provided for open, competitive exams for applicants for government jobs classified under civil service and banned the practice of exacting political contributions from civil servants or otherwise pressing them into partisan service.

Commissioner Eaton accepted his appointment and moved into Wormley's Hotel. He and the other two commissioners met regularly in his third-floor suite until office space was secured. At the time only 13,780 jobs were covered by the act, yet what the commissioners brought about was the end of the spoils system, placing government employment on a competitive basis and halting the recurring mass exodus and influx of workers after every change of administration. While they worked out details of implementing such sweeping changes as the Pendleton Act called for, Lord Coleridge, Chief Justice of England, also moved into Wormley's for an extended stay. His entourage occupied nine rooms that became the focal point of the comings and goings of President Arthur's cabinet members who called on the chief justice throughout his stay. The reception held for Lord Coleridge and the U.S. Supreme Court justices made for front-page newspaper stories in the United States and England, the best free advertising Wormley could wish for.

At some point during the year Wormley decided to donate his Henry Ulke portrait of Charles Sumner to the State of Massachusetts for the State House in Boston. A letter from Henry Pierce, a member of the House of Representatives from Massachusetts during the 43rd and 44th Congresses and a former resident of Wormley's, wrote a letter dated September 26, 1883, to thank the hotelier. In some ways the Ulke portrait was Wormley's most generous gift, especially in light of recent challenges to the legal status of Negroes.

Sumner's posthumous civil rights bill had passed in 1875. Its purpose was to protect all citizens in places of public accommodation throughout the United States. In some places Negroes were served without incident. In others the Civil Rights Act was blatantly ignored. When lawsuits initiated by colored persons began to reach the Supreme Court, the justices chose representative cases as a basis for a decision in 1883. Because the Supreme Court had already circumscribed the Fourteenth Amendment by strictly limiting its application to actual state violations of due process and equal protection in 1876 in the Cruikshank and Reese cases, bad news in the colored community should have come as no surprise. But the decision stunned Negroes across the country, James Wormley of Washington no exception. Justice Bradley, who had provided the eighth and deciding vote in each of the Electoral Commission disputes, spoke for the court when he struck down the Civil Rights Act of 1875, returning to the states the responsibility for safeguarding civil liberties generally and in places of public accommodation specifically. As Bradley put it, "individual invasion of private rights" was not the objective of the Civil Rights Act. "It would be running the slavery argument into the ground to make it apply to every act of discrimination which a person may see fit to make as to the guests he will entertain, or as to the people he will take into his coach or cab or car; or admit to his concert or theater, or deal with other matters of intercourse or business."[10] Once again states' rights were in the ascendancy.

A Hayes appointee to the court was the lone dissenter. Kentuckian John Marshall Harlan made it unmistakably clear that "the substance and spirit of the recent amendments to the Constitution have been sacrificed by a subtle and verbal criticism."[11] Harlan ended his dissent with a warning that the United States had entered "an era of constitutional law, when the rights of freedom and American citizenship cannot receive from the nation that efficient protection which heretofore was unhesitatingly afforded to slavery."[12]

A few days after the announcement of the court decision more than two thousand Negroes jammed the District's Lincoln Hall. Frederick Douglass thundered that the decision "presents the United States before the world as a Nation utterly destitute of power to protect the rights of its own citizens upon its own soil. . . . In humiliating the colored people of this country, this decision has humbled the nation."[13] No colored person in the District missed the real meaning of the 1883 Supreme Court decision. The movement for equal status for Negroes had fizzled; hope was slowly transformed into disappointment, then despair. Not even the Supreme Court's subsequent and unanimous civil rights decision, *Ex Parte Yarbrough* (1884) lessened this despair.[14] In writing for the court, Justice Miller stated that federal law prohibited anyone to use "force, intimidation, or threat" to prevent another person from voting. The Fifteenth Amendment, he insisted, "does substantially confer on the Negro the right to vote and Congress has the power to protect and enforce that right." Though *Ex Parte Yarbrough* contradicts Miller's and other justices' interpretation of the Fourteenth Amendment in Slaughterhouse and of the Fifteenth Amendment in Reese, little attention was paid to this 1884 decision.

James Wormley buried his indignation in more hard work. At this very time the large German legation set up housekeeping in the hotel, and he was occupied managing its demands. Life went on like this for Wormley until the summer of 1884 when illness slowed him down. He suffered from calculus, an abnormal mass in the body, usually formed of mineral salts and found in the gallbladder, kidneys, or urinary bladder. Unable to stand the pain of what are today referred to as kidney stones, he checked into Boston's Massachusetts General for corrective surgery. On Wednesday, October 15, he was operated on and seemed to have come out of the ordeal in good shape. By Thursday evening, however, he worsened, having developed peritonitis in a medical era with no antibiotics; his family was summoned.

He died Saturday, October 18, at one in the afternoon. His body was shipped to Washington, where it lay in state in the Sumner parlor of the hotel. Obituaries praising his life's work appeared in newspapers in major cities across the land. The city's hotels flew their flags at half mast and their managers and owners paid tribute to their distinguished colleague at his funeral on Wednesday, October 22, at two p.m. Three clergymen, one Baptist, and two Presbyterian, officiated; distinguished men, white and colored, served as pallbearers, including the manager of the Ebbitts Hotel; directors of the Arlington and Willard Hotels; John Cook Jr., black superintendent of the colored schools; and Blanche Bruce, Negro ex-senator from Mississippi. Wormley was buried in a red cedar casket under a monument that cost $755 in the Columbian Harmony Cemetery. He left his heirs—wife, four children, and twenty-five grandchildren—an estimated $150,000, a fortune in 1884 dollars.[15]

Three days later a story appeared in the Cleveland *Plain Dealer,* headlined "Wealthy Washingtonians." The unnamed reporter, who had obviously not kept up with the paper's obituaries, began with James Wormley, "the proprietor of the now far-famed Wormley Hotel. He is called the richest colored man here. I am told that $150,000 is a fair estimate. It is mostly in real property. For magnificence of entertainment his hotel ranks among the finest in the United States, and his patrons are solely such men as [James] Blaine, [Roscoe] Conkling, and [Frederick] Frelinghuysen. He is one of the most enterprising citizens here, and his commercial paper is as good as gold in the money market and, although quite modest, wields an immense influence."[16]

In 1885 William H. A. Wormley, the oldest of James's children, petitioned the school board to name the newly built elementary school in Georgetown the Wormley School in honor of his father's contributions to public school education.[17] Because he had chaired the building committee that oversaw the construction of the Sumner School in 1872—it was Sumner who had recommended Wormley as trustee of the Colored School Board—the 1885 school board acted on William's petition and named the new school on Prospect Street after the hotelier. The Wormley Public Elementary School for the Colored remained an all-black school in the District of Columbia's segregated system until 1952.[18]

An advertisement announcing an auction at Wormley's stables in the alley bounded by I and K and Fifteenth and Sixteenth Streets appeared in the *Washington Post* on May 27, 1885. Billed as a "fine opportunity to secure first-class outfits as Mr. Wormley was always noted for his stylish Horses and Carriages," the auction took place on June 2.[19] Fifteen horses, three landaus, one cart, one Victoria, a six-passenger hotel coach, a market wagon, three sleighs, as well as saddles, harnesses, and the like, were sold. The money realized from the auction became part of the inventory of the estate, filed on November 30 and notarized December 11. The inventory, dozens of pages in length, listed all goods, chattels, and personal items of James Wormley, including carpets, pillows, mattresses (hair and husk), furniture, towel racks, washstands, urns, pedestals, 3,662 bottles of assorted liquors, 36 gallons of sherry, 36 gallons of whiskey, hundreds of chairs, tables, chandeliers, and an accounting of the bills James Wormley had paid shortly before his death such as for the Chesapeake and Potomac Telephone Company, plumbing, gas fixtures, elevator equipment and inspection, fish, game, butter, glassware, meats, paint, tin work, horseshoeing, and the like.[20]

As William Wormley, the estate's executor, worked diligently on the inventory, Henry Ulke painted James Wormley's portrait, using a photograph that he had taken himself. Ulke's photographic studio on Pennsylvania Avenue came to rival Matthew Brady's, but as popular as photographic portraiture was, Ulke became better known for his oil portraits, which projected the instantaneous quality of a photograph. Small wonder that Ulke was in such demand. The Wormley portrait conveys the hotelier's self-confident and affable personality, and by using the then fashionable Rembrandt-like, chiaroscuro technique, namely strong lighting on the subject's face against a dark background, Ulke achieved a striking effect. When he finished, the portrait was displayed in a prominent place in the newly named Wormley School.[21]

After the inventory had been notarized, Anna Wormley, who had moved out to the Tenleytown property, and her daughter, Anna, sold their shares of the hotel to William, James T., and Garrett Smith. A short two years later William Wormley advertised in the *Star*:

> Country real estate: FOR SALE-B I have one or two of the prettiest and most complete country homes in the District, Just in the rear of the President's home [Cleveland] on Pierce Mill Road. Will sell one or both; large houses on both places, 10 and 11 rooms each, with pantry, bath-rooms . . . hot and cold water supply; fruits of all kind, and good stables.[22]

At the same time this ad appeared, William and Garrett sold their portion of the business to James T., who remained the sole proprietor of the hotel until it was sold in December 1893 to Charles Gibbs, former manager of the Ebbitt House, who continued to operate it under the Wormley name until 1897.[23]

James T. Wormley's decision to sell had been a pragmatic one. Even after such a demoralizing development as the Supreme Court decision of 1883, an old, well-established family like the Wormleys, James T. might have reasoned, could weather the storm. But the defeat of the elections bill of 1890 disabused him of such a notion. When Republicans won back both houses of Congress for the first time since 1872 in the election of 1888, Sen. Henry Cabot Lodge of Massachusetts introduced an elections bill, or the Force Bill, as it came to be known. The bill proposed to give federal supervisors power to control registration and pass on the qualifications of challenged voters. Though he initially believed the Republican Party was in a position to enforce the Fourteenth and Fifteenth Amendments, Lodge discovered he was sadly mistaken. Too many of his Senate colleagues had a greater interest in high tariff and silver bills than in providing federal supervision over federal elections in the South. And anyway, these colleagues believed, a revival of Reconstruction tactics might disrupt business that had developed between North and South. Wormley could not have known that the 1890 elections bill would be the last attempt to protect civil rights of Negroes for more than half a century, but he surely sensed the inevitable outcome of the near-total disenfranchisement of Negroes that had occurred in the nine years since his father's death, resulting in an almost complete separation of the races. Accordingly, he and his brothers sold off the last of the three Wormley houses in Tenleytown in 1894.

Southern Redeemers, on the other hand, saw the Lodge Bill, defeated though it had been, as a threat. Convinced that Republicans meant to renew Reconstruction, they moved fast to exclude the Negro completely and permanently from politics. They started with voting. South Carolina passed an "eight-box" law that required voters to deposit votes for various offices in separate ballot boxes. Since this was in effect a literacy test, many Negro voters were thereby disenfranchised. Georgia required a payment of a poll tax. Between 1889 and 1902, every former Confederate state followed Georgia's example and imposed a poll tax as a prerequisite to voting: South Carolina in 1895; Louisiana in 1898; North Carolina in 1900; Alabama in 1901; and Virginia in 1902. Additionally, Louisiana, North Carolina, Alabama, and Georgia also enacted "grandfather" clauses that allowed men to vote only if they could prove that they or their ancestors had voted before 1867, the year that Negroes had been franchised.[24]

Then in 1896, in *Plessy v. Ferguson*, the Supreme Court sanctioned another dimension of second-class citizenship, this one worse than the first. Homer Plessy, seven-eighths white and one-eighth colored man, tried to sit in a railroad coach

reserved for whites. Plessy was arrested because of an 1890 Louisiana law that separated railroad coaches by race. Plessy fought his arrest all the way to Supreme
Court. The majority decision in *Plessy v. Ferguson* established the concept of "separate but equal," which meant that states could legally segregate races in any public accommodations, from railroad cars to schools, from streetcars to water
fountains, from restaurants to restrooms. The court thereby put a seal of approval
on Jim Crow segregation, the American version of apartheid.[25] As in 1883, John
Marshall Harlan wrote the only dissenting opinion.

After *Plessy v. Ferguson*, life turned brutal for the Negro. While the federal government stood by, an average of one hundred Negroes a year were lynched, with
no attempt to bring participants to justice.[26] Nor did the Justice Department in-
terfere with the new practice of leasing convicts to private contractors like coal-
mining firms, railroad construction companies, and planters, which was
widespread throughout the South. The practice was fabulously lucrative—no
housing or food costs for prisoners plus states received income from leasing. A
steady stream of convicts, 90 percent of whom were colored, was made possible
by broad new vagrancy laws that permitted the arrest of any jobless person.
Moreover, criminal laws increased sharply for petty theft. The labor these men
provided came cheaply, cheaper even than slaves, who had to be fed and clothed.

These former slaves provided another source of cheap labor. Because agriculture
had made a dramatic recovery, it dominated the labor scene. The planting aristocracy, as in pre-Civil War times, operated their plantations with former slaves who
worked the land as tenant farmers, splitting the crop with the owner, who also provided seed and supplies at a price he set, payable in crops. Somehow the sharecrop-
pers never seemed to earn enough to pay off their debts to the landowners. The *New
National Era* reported this scandal in a piece that appeared on October 3, 1872.

The Southern gentleman rents the land to his former slave at about the
whole value of the land each year, and thus practically sells his land each
year, recovering it at the end. This high-toned gentleman, this soul of honor,
does more—he "furnishes" the people on his plantation, buys provisions,
and sells to the poor colored man at an advance of 50 to 100 percent, agreeing to wait until the crop is picked out and ready for market. A little judi-
cious exaggeration of the account usually attends these operations, and at the
end of the year, the colored man frequently finds that he has nothing due
him for his year's labor.[27]

Sharecropping was essentially slavery under a new name. Negroes, as a result of convict leasing and sharecropping, composed a huge disenfranchised class of dependent laborers. Although they represented a big proportion of the nation's laboring population, they were essentially invisible because they were without legal rights. Their absence from public life shifted the center of gravity of American politics to the right. The solid South, conservative Democrat without the freedmen, weakened any prospects of change in racial matters or, for that matter, any prospects of progressive legislation in any matter. The Southern conservative redeemers henceforth increasingly aligned themselves with those Northern Republicans who sought to further the ends of commerce and thwart labor activism. These former enemies became a political coalition and together became a support instead of a threat to the new social order of a rising industrialism and to a court system that gave property rights precedence over civil rights.

The one area of hope was the cohesive, well-organized, elite black community of the District. These Negroes' strong sense of solidarity was to serve them well during the long wait for better days. When these better days finally came, and the Legal Defense Fund set about dismantling Jim Crow laws in the 1960s, the example of James Wormley's efforts was helpful. The so-called "lost laws," anti-discrimination statutes passed during Reconstruction with Wormley's help through his influential Massachusetts friends, played a major role in the Fund's dismantling of the District's segregation.[28]

By the time William McKinley, the last Civil War soldier to serve as president, had acquiesced to a congressional declaration of war with Spain in April 1898 over Cuban independence, sectional reconciliation was all but complete, albeit at the price of racial equality. The sons of the Blue and Gray fought together, serving the cause of reconciliation by uniting North and South against a common external foe. Although 10,000 Negroes enlisted and served in the forces that fought in the Spanish-American War, segregation, sharecropping, convict-leasing, and lynching continued unabated.

As Civil War veterans aged and began to die, reunions of the Blue and Gray multiplied and became commonplace all over the country. During the administration of the first Southern president since the Civil War, the fiftieth anniversary of the battle of Gettysburg was celebrated. Woodrow Wilson, the president who segregated federal offices and whose favorite film was *Birth of a Nation*, a movie that glorified the Ku Klux Klan, spoke before a reunion of 50,000 Union and Confederate veterans at Gettysburg. Celebrating the reconciliation of sections, he intoned, "How wholesome and healing the peace has been." There was no healing for those Negro veterans still alive, whose service was ignored even though 200,000 black men had served in the Civil War. Not one colored veteran appeared on the reunion program, and not one word was uttered about their sacrifice fifty years earlier on that very ground as servants for officers and later as combatants. The new nation Lincoln had brought into being at that very place in 1863 when he said that the United States was founded on the "proposition that all men are created equal" had disappeared by 1913.

White supremacy reigned supreme until almost a century after the "official" end of Reconstruction in 1877. Not until President Eisenhower sent federal troops to Little Rock in 1957 to enforce the *Brown v. Board of Education* decision the Supreme Court made three years earlier did the second era of Civil Rights begin in earnest. That the changes wrought by the Civil War and Reconstruction lasted such a pitifully short time leads to the logical question—who really won the Civil War? Such a state of affairs would not have been possible without the quiet acquiescence of the North. Commercial motives account for the powerful impetus to reconciliation, even at the cost of a strong federal government protecting civil rights for the Negro, but post-war historians did much to justify Northern indifference to the nullification of the Fourteenth and Fifteenth Amendments.

James Ford Rhodes wrote a seven-volume *History of the United States from the Compromise of 1850* between 1893 and 1906. Although an amateur historian in the sense that he started his literary work after a successful business career in coal mining, his interpretation of the Civil War—he removed blame and praised soldiers' valor on both sides—and of Reconstruction—he called it "the oppression of the South by the North" and chastised Radical Republicans for misunderstanding race—set a formula for twentieth-century historians. Most influential of these was William A. Dunning, a popular history professor at Columbia University in the early years of the twentieth century, who turned out scores of PhDs in history. They in turn promulgated Lost Cause mythology, teaching and writing that African Americans were children incapable of understanding or appreciating the suffrage the North thrust upon them, and that Southern whites knew best how to deal with them. Not until the mid-twentieth century civil rights revolution did revisionist historians appear on the scene, men like C. Vann Woodward, Keith Ian Polakoff, and Eric Foner, who showed that even if Reconstruction in the South was sometimes marred by corruption, it implemented progressive changes like rebuilding the South's shattered infrastructure, establishing the region's first public school systems and passing laws to guarantee equal civil and political rights for all Americans, even Negroes.

Between 1865 and 1870 an amazing body of law, the Thirteenth, Fourteenth, and Fifteenth Amendments together with the civil rights and enforcement legislation, created a new constitution that extended to Negroes full rights of citizenship, established for the first time in U.S. history a constitutional guarantee to equality, and empowered the federal government to protect the fundamental rights of its citizens. These laws gave Washington power over matters that had, since the end of the Federalist era in 1803, been the sole jurisdiction of the states. But three Supreme Court cases emasculated Reconstruction's amendments, a devastating development since Congress had placed the burden of enforcing freedmen's civil rights on the federal judiciary. Worse, by disarming those trying to maintain black access to the ballot, these decisions brought on the most serious electoral crisis ever to confront the nation. Not until the civil rights revolution of the late 1950s and 1960s did the Supreme Court uphold congressional laws reestablishing the primacy of the Union in protecting citizens' civil rights. The Rehnquist Court, however, swung to a states' rights revolution, and what is most surprising was the majority justices' particular respect for the decisions of 1873, 1876, and 1883.[29] Time will tell, but the Roberts Court seems even more conservative than its predecessor.

The tragic past keeps coming back.

EPILOGUE:
THEN AND NOW

*T*he period we live in today is alarmingly similar to the last quarter of the nineteenth century in several striking ways. Big money has not held all the cards as it does today since the Gilded Age of the late nineteenth and early twentieth centuries. The United States, then and now, has arguably the most unequal distribution of wealth in the Western world.[1] In the last two decades especially, tectonic shifts have taken place in the division between the haves and have-nots. Newport-like mansions have made a comeback, spouting architects like Thierry Despont, to name an example, who specialize in designing houses from 20,000 to 60,000 square feet for the super rich. Armies of servants and gargantuan yachts are back as well. Shocking corporate corruption at Enron, Arthur Andersen, WorldCom, Adelphia, AIG, Bernard Madoff's firm, and on and on, look much like the Crédit Mobilier and Emma Mines affairs, the whiskey frauds, and post tradership turpitude. In retrospect the four decades of New Deal/Fair Deal innovations like banking and investment regulation, social security, and the G.I. Bill and the Great Society's civil rights legislation, look like a middle-class refuge between two lengthy gilded eras. In order that a total nonregulation in economic matters comes to pass, a huge and strong network of libertarian public-interest lawyers, scholars, and sympathetic activist judges urge conservatives to use the courts to strike down any remaining vestiges of the New Deal. One of this network, Michael Greve of the American Enterprise Institute, argues that the twenty-first century's "modern, vibrant, mobile" global economy is competitive enough to regulate itself.[2] Yet we see at the end of the new century's first decade how far off the mark such a conclusion really is.

Consider also how alike the elections of 1876 and 2000 were, even to the detail of Florida. Like Samuel Tilden in 1876, Al Gore won the popular vote, receiving 539,898 votes more than George W. Bush. The popular vote gave Gore 266 electoral votes to Bush's 246. The state of Florida, with 25 electoral votes, was too close to call. Since there are 538 electoral votes in the fifty states and the District of Columbia, and to be elected president, a candidate must win at least 50 percent plus one, or 270 electoral votes, whoever won Florida won the election. As Bush received Florida's votes, he won the election by one electoral vote, that is, 271 electoral votes.[3]

Katherine Harris, who was both secretary of state of Florida in charge of elections and George W. Bush's Florida campaign chairman—think of her as a one-person Returning Board—paid $4 million to Database Technologies to go through Florida's voter rolls and remove former felons, as Florida law bars felons from voting. The problem arose when her office instructed Database, in order not to chance missing any guilty individual, to exclude even people with names and social security numbers similar to known felons. Database complied and as a result deleted 173,000 registered voters from the voter rolls. On Election Day, November 7, 2000, hundreds of law-abiding citizens were not allowed to vote, these mostly in black and Hispanic communities. Since Bush was officially credited with receiving 537 more votes than Al Gore in Florida, it is possible, even probable, the voters barred from voting because of deletion from the voter rolls would have made the difference.

Once again, as in 1876 when John Reid, managing editor of the *New York Time*, called the election in doubt in the early morning papers, a call that emboldened Zachary Chandler to declare Hayes the electoral victor, so too John Ellis, Bush's first cousin and the man in charge of the election night desk for Fox News, decided to go on the air and declare Bush the winner before the counting of the votes had been completed. The other networks followed Fox's lead and declared Bush the president-elect.

Meanwhile arguments ensued about the counting or recounting of votes actually cast. Tens of thousands of ballots were tossed out because of a wrongly placed or stray mark, dimpled chads, hanging chads, and other seeming irregularities. On Friday, December 8, the Florida Supreme Court ordered a manual recount of all disputed ballots, about 60,000, throughout the state. "The manual recount was progressing smoothly," the *New York Times* reported on December 9, "with new votes being recorded for both Vice President Al Gore and Gov. George W. Bush." Eighty county judges were able to go through more than a third of the nine thousand Miami-Dade County ballots being recounted, to take the example of one county. They expected to finish by nightfall. Bush appealed to the Supreme Court to stop the recount. Mid-afternoon December 9 the court accepted Bush's appeal and by a 5–4 vote granted Bush's request to stop the recount. When the recount stopped, Gore was trailing Bush by sixty-six votes.

Both Gore and Bush filed briefs on December 10, and the case was argued on December 11. On December 12 the Court ruled, 5–4, that the recount as structured by the Florida Supreme Court was unconstitutional and that there was no time to fix it. The majority's argument cited a violation of the equal protection clause of the Fourteenth Amendment, namely that because of the different ways of determining the voters' intent in the Florida counties, voters were treated unequally. If the majority were consistent, however, it would have had to invalidate all of Florida since the methods of voting and counting votes varied all over the state. For that matter, different methods of counting votes exist throughout the fifty states. Texas, for instance, counts dimpled chads; California does not. Moreover, forty-four of fifty states do not have uniform voting methods, and voting machines do not work the same way for all states. So, to rule as the majority of the Supreme Court ruled, that having differing standards for counting votes violates the equal protection clause, these justices necessarily invalidated all elections throughout the country. That is why, no doubt, the court's majority wrote that this ruling that conferred the presidency on Bush was "limited to the present circumstances, for the problem of equal protection in election processes generally presents many complexities." Obviously the majority knew its decision was not based on the merits of the law.

Making the partisan nature of this decision even more apparent is the time issue. Since the electors in the fifty states were not to meet until December 18, if the majority had really believed that the various standards in the various counties to determine a voter's intent violated the equal protection clause, why not, as justices Stevens, Souter, Ginsburg, and Breyer noted in their dissents, simply remand the case back to the Supreme Court with instructions to establish a uniform, statewide standard and continue the recount until December 18.

The Fourteenth Amendment was an odd choice for this particular court to have used for Bush's defense, as the majority of justices had disclaimed equal protection when used by individuals who sought to halt discrimination based on race. In fact, a cohesive 5–4 majority has, since the mid-1990s, been enhancing the power of the states at the expense of the federal government and, in this respect, is most disquietingly a copy of the late-nineteenth century Supreme Court.

The Rehnquist Court's five-member majority in a series of decisions shifted the balance of power from Congress (the federal government) to the states. Like the post-Reconstruction Supreme Court that increasingly ruled against federal authority and in favor of states' rights, so too the Rehnquist Court steadily expanded states' immunity from the reach of federal law in several 5–4 decisions. In 2002 John T. Noonan Jr., a Reagan appointee to the Ninth U.S. Circuit Court of Appeals, came out with a book called *Narrowing the Nation's Power: The Supreme Court Sides with the States.* In it he says that these five justices have "return[ed] the country to a pre-Civil War understanding of the nation."[4] But President Lincoln and three Reconstruction amendments had changed the way people thought about the Constitution. For states' rights advocates, or as they are sometimes called, "original intent" advocates, what Lincoln said and Radical Republicans did had misdirected American governance. Yet what Lincoln said and the Radical Republicans did in passing the three Reconstruction amendments made James Wormley's success possible not only for himself and his family. By managing rooming houses and a catering business, by building and running the District's most luxurious hotel, by buying and operating Wormley's Clubhouse with its spacious stables and race track for horse owners to train horses, he also created jobs for many, many others. Despite several Reconstruction successes, a considerable number of people remained skeptical of federal power but not state power.

The 5–4 majority of the Rehnquist Court in several cases declared the states beyond the reach of many federal laws, granting them what lawyers call "sovereign immunity." Its mantra that the "states entered the union with their sovereignty intact" has no basis in the text or history of the Constitution, before or after 1789. Only one historically significant document, the Constitution of the Confederate States of America, reflects this view. The U.S. Constitution, which begins "We the people of the United States," is ambiguous when it comes to federal-state confrontations. The Confederate constitution had no such ambiguity about the locus of sovereignty: "We, the people of the Confederate states, each state acting in its sovereign and independent character."

Immunity is a common law doctrine. John Marshall, chief justice of the Supreme Court from 1801 until 1835 and the court's dominant influence during its early and formative years, held that immunity was waived by the states as to federal questions when the states ratified the Constitution. Nothing supports the view that immunity was part of the constitutional design.

The U.S. Constitution's Eleventh Amendment does, however, expressly recognize a partial version of sovereign immunity for the states. It prohibits citizens from suing a state in federal court, unless the state is their own. Thus, a citizen of Louisiana, for instance, can sue the state of Louisiana in federal court but cannot sue the state of Virginia there. The purpose of the amendment goes back to the *Chisholm v. Georgia* decision in 1793, the Supreme Court's first foray into constitutional law. In 1792 Alexander Chisholm, a citizen of South Carolina, filed suit against the state of Georgia. Chisholm was acting as executor of the estate of Robert Farquhar, who had sold uniforms to Georgia during the Revolution but was never paid. Georgia's attorney general responded in federal district court that his "sovereign" state was immune to suit by citizens of other states. The case wound up in the Supreme Court. Chisholm hired Attorney General Edmund Randolph to represent him as a private lawyer. Randolph argued that Article III of the Constitution gave the Supreme Court jurisdiction over "controversies between a state and citizens of another state."[5] The Constitution, he continued, had replaced the Articles of Confederation, so it was now the people of the United States, not the individual states, who were sovereign. Justice James Wilson, who had played a leading role in drafting Article III at the Philadelphia convention, was the court's leading advocate of federal precedence over the states. "As to the purpose of the Union," he wrote in his thirty-page opinion, "Georgia is not a sovereign state."[6] Other justices concurred. The states reacted with ferocious anger; within days of the decision in February 1793, Virginia and Massachusetts petitioned Congress to forge an amendment to overturn the Court's ruling. Other states followed their lead. The furor refused to die down, so even though Federalists controlled both houses of Congress, they did adopt the Eleventh Amendment in March 1794. "Judicial power of the United States," it said, did not extend to suits "against one of the United States by citizens of another State" or by subjects of foreign nations. The amendment was ratified in 1798.

Under Article I, section 8 of the Constitution, Congress has authority to regulate interstate commerce, coin money, establish military defense, grant patents, but not to protect citizens of the respective states from discrimination by their own states. After the Civil War, however, the Fourteenth Amendment filled that gap. The Fourteenth Amendment declares that born or naturalized Americans have, in effect, dual citizenship; they are citizens of the state of their residence and also of the United States. Accordingly, it proscribes states from making laws that violate the rights of citizens of the United States and requires that they give each citizen "equal protection of the laws."

Finally, section 5 of the Fourteenth Amendment empowers Congress to make laws to enforce these guarantees. Before the Rehnquist court, the Supreme Court had left it up to Congress to decide for itself what legislation was "appropriate." This is no longer so; now the Court decides what legislation is appropriate for Congress to pass. The Rehnquist court said that to "validate" a law enacted under section 5, "there must be congruence and proportionality between the injury to be prevented or remedied and the means adopted to that end."[7] In other words, Congress must establish a documentary record that a national evil exists before Congress can legislate to protect life, liberty, or property under the Fourteenth Amendment. Without this history of "widespread and persisting" deprivation of rights, states can lose immunity against suit. The minority of the court, dissenting justices Breyer, Ginsburg, Souter, and Stevens, pointed to a serious breach in the separation-of-powers principle on which the federal government rests.

In his book, Judge Noonan says the court has taken this doctrine of sovereign immunity to extremes, and in so doing all but rewrites the Eleventh Amendment. While this amendment concerns suits against state governments, the Rehnquist Court also applied it to state-sponsored activities, and Noonan cites a series of decisions to prove his point. The case of an author of a collection of short stories who sued an academic press for violating her copyright, for example, was thrown out of court on the grounds that the press was part of a university, the university was part of a state, and the state was immune to Congress's copyright statute. There are real victims when national power is restricted: a professor who was fired for discriminatory reasons by a state university, a nursing supervisor whose salary was cut when she was stricken by breast cancer, and a freshman student who invoked the Violence Against Women Act after being repeatedly raped by two of her college's football players and unable to persuade her school to take the crime seriously.

The Supreme Court's decisions prompted the Senate Judiciary Committee to hold a hearing on what then chairman Patrick Leahy, Democrat of Vermont, called this "unrelenting assault" by the U.S. Supreme Court on the legislative powers of Congress.[8] "In a series of five-to-four decisions, the Court's so-called 'conservative' wing radically altered the balance of power between the Congress and the states," Leahy said on the floor of the Senate on October 1, 2000, "greatly restricting our ability to protect the individual rights and liberties of ordinary Americans." Worse, he continued, the court's decisions were not based on the text of the Constitution or on precedent but on "broad abstract notions of 'state sovereignty.'" Leahy began expressing his concerns about the court's new direction in July 1999 after it issued its end-of-term decisions in *Florida Prepaid v. College Savings Bank.* In these cases the court ruled that states could not be held liable for violating federal intellectual property laws. Charles Fried, former solicitor general during the Reagan administration, called these decisions "truly bizarre."[9] Senator Arlen Specter, then Republican of Pennsylvania, remarked that they "leave us with an absurd and untenable state of affairs."[10]

A year later Leahy went to the floor of the Senate to discuss still more 5–4 decisions, namely *Kimel v. Florida Board of Regents*, a decision that held state employees are not protected by the federal law banning age discrimination, and *United States v. Morrison*, a decision that invalidated a portion of the Violence Against Women Act of 1994 that provided a federal remedy for victims of sexual assault and violence. And again the following year, Leahy said, "the Court continued its state sovereignty crusade" in the *Board of Trustees of the University of Alabama v. Garrett* case. The plaintiff in *Garrett* was a nurse at the University of Alabama who had been diagnosed with breast cancer and was demoted after taking sick leave to undergo surgery and chemotherapy. The court held that state employees could no longer enforce their right not to be discriminated against under the Americans with Disabilities Act. "The Rehnquist Court," Leahy concluded, "has embarked on a path of sacrificing the legal rights of individuals in favor of what it calls 'dignity' of the states. . . . There is ample dignity in adherence to law."[11]

The Supreme Court's minority sharply disagreed with the majority's historical and conceptual understanding of sovereignty. The majority, they said, elevates sovereignty over justice, and if sovereign immunity shields states in both federal and state courts, it violates a principle "much closer to the hearts of the framers: that where there is a right, there must be a remedy."[12] In their written dissent to a ruling the majority made that rejected a suit by probation officers against the state of Maine for violating federal law on overtime pay, they quoted the opinion of Chief Justice John Marshall in *Marbury v. Madison.* "The very essence of civil liberty certainly consists in the right of every individual to claim protection of the laws, whenever he receives an injury. . . . In Great Britain the King himself is sued in the respectful form of a petition, and he never fails to comply with the judgment of his court." This same principle is enshrined in modern international human rights law.

The Rehnquist Court's states' rights agenda was a long time in the making. William Rehnquist had been a justice of the Supreme Court fourteen years when he was made chief justice in 1986. At that time he openly declared his agenda for the court: to return power to the states. A states' rights agenda within the Supreme Court is likely to last a long time as well. President Bush filled two vacancies on the court with justices both young and conservative who will likely sit on the bench for thirty years or more. His federal and appellate nominees tended to be young and conservative as well. Yet history clearly shows that justice cannot be left to the states alone; states have violated federal laws, which is precisely why Congress, after the Civil War, enacted the Fourteenth Amendment. But the raison d'être of immunity is to shield not only state governments but also many subsidiary state agencies from complying with federal laws enacted for the good of all. In light of these states' rights decisions, how deeply ironic and disillusioning, then, is the court's majority ruling in *Bush v. Gore* in which the national court intruded upon state sovereignty.

This new activism threatens not only top-down, Washington-centric, New Deal–type programs, but also contemporary centrist initiatives that deploy federal funds and impose federal standards to remedy chronic shortcomings of local governments. As Chief Justice Rehnquist wrote in the 1995 case *Lopez v. United States*, which struck down the Gun-Free School Zones Act, there are areas over which the states "historically have been sovereign" and which, therefore, "the states may regulate but Congress may not."[13] The Supreme Court's majority repeatedly defines such off-limits areas to include education, law enforcement, and family policy— all targets for broadly popular contemporary reform efforts.

Paul Gewirtz, a professor of law at Yale, and Chad Golder, a 2005 graduate of Yale Law School, studied how often Supreme Court justices have struck down congressional law on constitutional grounds, the boldest act of judges since Congress is an elected legislative body representing the entire nation. According to Gewirtz and Golder, since the first session of the Supreme Court justices have struck down an average of one congressional statute every two years. Calling congressional legislation into question when it is unconstitutional is one thing, but a marked increase occurred after 1994. Between 1994 and 2005 the Rehnquist Court struck down thirty-three federal laws on constitutional grounds. Justices Breyer, Ginsburg, Souter, and Stevens, those considered the more liberal justices, voted least frequently to overturn congressional statutes. Those justices labeled conservative voted more frequently to do so, and by this measure they were the more activist judges. And yet, what many see as a states' rights revolution in the court was decidedly undercut by the 2005 *Gonzales v. Raich* 6–3 ruling upholding the power of Congress to ban and prosecute the possession and use of marijuana for medical purposes, even in the eleven states that permit it. Still, now that Justice O'Connor, an occasional swing vote, has retired and Justice Rehnquist has died, it is becoming clear that George W. Bush succeeded where his father and Reagan failed: in nominating John Roberts as chief justice and Samuel Alito as Justice O'Connor's replacement, Bush finally achieved a distinctly right-wing, ideological court.

"It's not often in law that so few have changed so much so quickly," Justice Stephen Breyer said, referring to several aggressive 5–4 opinions that overturned precedents. The court overruled Congress by nullifying a key part of the McCain-Feingold campaign finance law, a law designed to reduce the role of special interest money in politics. It overturned the policies of federal agencies like the Equal Employment Opportunity Commission, making it difficult, if not impossible, for many victims of discrimination to prevail by severely limiting a worker's window for filing a wage discrimination claim. It overturned a ninety-six-year-old precedent under which it was illegal for a manufacturer and retailer to collude on minimum resale prices. In another 5–4 decision, the justices threw out a separation-of-church-and-state lawsuit filed against President Bush's faith-based social services initiative. And their last decision of the 2007 session, *Parents Involved in Community Schools v. Seattle District No. 1*, signals a complete departure from more than half a century of decisions on race. The court decreed that Seattle and Louisville and hundreds of other cities and counties had to stop their integration programs. By a vote of 5–4 they said that using a student's race to govern the availability of a place at a desired school, even for the purpose of preventing re-segregation, violated the Fourteenth Amendment's guarantee of equal protection. Arguing that the Fourteenth Amendment protects society from integration is reminiscent of the reasoning in the Rehnquist's 5–4 decision in *Bush v. Gore* in 2000. In an early decision in 2010 the court, by permitting businesses and unions to spend freely on commercials for or against candidates, ended decades-old restrictions. Besides pushing hard on finance issues during the 2009–2010 term, Chief Justice Roberts led 5–4 decisions on gun rights by restraining the federal government's ability to significantly limit "the right to keep and bear arms," and restricted the "honest services" criminal fraud law to cover only bribes and kickbacks, eliminating a range of illicit activities prosecutors have used to convict dishonest white-collar workers. Sen. Patrick Leahy criticized the court for disregarding "the will of Congress and undermining efforts to protect Americans from abuses by powerful corporate and political interests."[14]

American law has truly undergone a transformation in recent years, shifting its focus away from broad principles of fairness and toward a willingness to subject people to treatment that might be unjust on the grounds that it is legal. In the rights revolution of the 1960s the Supreme Court found broad fairness principles in the Constitution and brought these to every part of society. The pendulum has swung back toward strict rules. Early in 2003 the court considered the case of Leandro Andrade, a father of three who, because of California's three-strikes-you're-out law, was sentenced to fifty years to life for stealing $153.54 worth of video tapes. The minority protested the unfairness of the sentence, arguing that it was "grossly disproportionate" to the crime, and therefore a violation of the Eighth Amendment's bar on cruel and unusual punishment. The majority concluded that rules are rules, and that the sentence "was not an unreasonable application of clearly established law."

The Reconstruction historian Eric Foner commented on the court's backward-looking positions. "If the Civil Rights movement of the 1950s and 1960s was often called the Second Reconstruction, we now seem to have entered a Second Redemption, as the restoration of white supremacy was called in the late-nineteenth century South. Just as the Supreme Court slowly eviscerated the legal structure of the First Reconstruction, . . . this Court is doing the same for the Second."[15]

In the past, the last morning of the Supreme Court's completed session has been the occasion for the announcement of a justice's retirement. No such announcement was forthcoming in 2008, an election year. In 2009 Judge Souter surprised everyone by announcing his intention of retiring. Barack Obama, elected president in 2008, nominated Sonia Sotomayor, who was then confirmed. John Paul Stevens, at age eighty-nine, surprised few when he announced his intention of retiring at the end of the 2010 session. President Obama nominated Elena Kagan, former policy adviser to former president Clinton, dean of the Harvard Law School, and solicitor general for President Obama, to replace Justice Stevens in the 2010–2011 court that reconvened in the fall. Kagan was confirmed in August. But two "liberals" replacing two equally "liberal" jurists will do nothing to change the direction of the court.

And so goes the recurring American story. Because the Constitution institutionalized a system of divided sovereignty, the seesaw between states' righters and federalists continues into the twenty-first century.

NOTES

$\mathscr{B}$ecause the reader will find detailed citations in the following notes for the books, articles, reports, newspapers, letters, journals, and archives I consulted and the interviews I conducted, I have omitted a formal bibliography. I owe a special thank-you to Mrs. Stanton Wormley (Freida), who not only shared her husband's multi-volume collection of scrapbooks that were in her home, she also allowed me to take whatever I needed out of her safekeeping to have various photocopies made, and, to add to her generous hospitality, she fed me during the many days I sat in her sunroom going through the seventy-three large scrapbooks. Recently these have been put on three CD-ROMs and can be consulted at the Historical Society of Washington, D.C. Freida Wormley was the widow of Stanton Wormley, who descended from James Wormley through the William Henry Ashburton Wormley line. She died in November of 2010 at the age of 88. Her husband, Stanton Wormley, and their son, Stanton Wormley Jr., with Paul E. Sluby Sr., compiled the family genealogy that has been privately printed.

Preface

1   See Stephen Goode, *The New Federalism—States Rights in American History* (New York: Franklin Watts, 1983), 145.

2   Eric Foner, *A Short History of Reconstruction, 1863–1877* (New York: HarperCollins, 1990), 247.

Chapter 1. What Might Have Been

1   Gore Vidal, *1876: A Novel* (New York: Random House, 1976), 147.

2   Ibid., 178.

3   *Wormeley-Wormley, ca. 1160–1991: The Father-to-Son Lineage of Stanton L. Wormley, Jr.*, compiled by Stanton L. Wormley Sr., Stanton L. Wormley Jr., and Paul E. Sluby Sr., privately printed, available at the Historical Society in Washington, D.C. (hereinafter cited as SLW Genealogy).

4   SLW Genealogy, vi.

5   Katherine Prescott Wormeley, Elizabeth Wormley Latimer, Ariana Randolph Wormley Curtis, *Recollections of Ralph Wormeley* (New York: privately printed, 1879), 4.

6   Information about Rosegill and its colonial occupants comes from the following: SLW Genealogy; Louise E. Gray, Evelyn Q. Ryland, Bettie J. Simmons, *Historic Buildings in Middlesex County, Virginia, 1650–1875* (Berryville, VA: Virginia Book Company, 1978); Reverend Horace Edwin Hayden, *Virginia Genealogies* (Washington, D.C.: Rare Book Shop, 1931); Wormeley et al., *Recollections*; *The Virginia Magazine of History and Biography* vol. 18 (for year ended 1910) and vol. 36 (for year ended 1928); and from author's observations during a visit to Urbanna, VA, in the summer of 2001.

7   Daniel Boorstin, *The Americans: The Colonial Experience* (New York: Vintage Books, 1958), 103.

8   Virginia Revere, "Know Your County," University of Virginia, 1935.

9   Gray et al., *Historic Buildings in Middlesex County*, 44.

10   Wormeley et al., *Recollections*, 10.

11   SLW Genealogy, 11.

12   Papers of Joseph Toner, Biographical File, Box 594, Library of Congress.

13   *The Virginia Magazine of History and Biography* vol. 18 (1910): 374.

14   1790 census.

15   Interview with Shirley Graves (Mrs. Donet), May 12, 2001; twenty-four slaves in 1806, Gray et al., *Historic Buildings in Middlesex County*.

16   Recollection of Mary Elizabeth Wormeley, later Mrs. Randolph Brandt Latimer, in a remembrance of her father, Rear Admiral Ralph Randolph Wormeley, and his times, 1850, Massachusetts Historical Society.

17   Mary Beth Corrigan, "Imaginary Cruelties? A History of the Slave Trade in Washington, D.C.," *Washington History* 13, no. 2 (Fall/Winter 2001–2002): 5.

18   Cheryl Miller, notes for "The Measure of a Man: James Wormley," an exhibit by the Historical Society of Washington, D.C. (1993).

19 Manumission was common in Virginia. After 1806, however, a manumitted slave could not remain in the state after twelve months. Lynch was twenty-six in 1806; since he remained in Virginia for another eight years, the probability is that he was either born free or manumitted at birth by his father. Luther Porter Jackson, "The Virginia Free Negro Farmer and Property Owner, 1830–1860," *Journal of Negro History* 24, no. 4 (October 1939): 391, 421.

20 Search conducted by Stanley Wormley, Sr. and Jr., and by Paul Sluby. Results can be found in the SLW Genealogy.

21 Tax ledger, RG41, National Archives.

22 Ralph Wormeley to Gov. Thomas Lee, December 1794; Ralph Wormley, addressee unknown, June 15, 1774. Wormley Papers, CD-ROM.

23 Dorothy Provine, "The Economic Position of Free Blacks in the District of Columbia, 1800–1860," *Journal of Negro History* 58 (January 1973): 61–72.

24 Paul Sluby, Index to Wills and Recorded 1801–1909, 1903, 1882, bk. 19, National Records Center, Suitland, MD, 461.

25 U.S. Department of Education, *Special Report of the Commissioner of Education on the Condition and Improvement of Public Schools in the District of Columbia*, submitted to the House of Representatives June 13, 1870, Government Printing Office, 1871.

26 Constance McLaughlin Green, *Washington: Village and Capital, 1800–1878* (Princeton, NJ: Princeton University Press, 1962).

27 Stephen B. Oates, ed., *The Approaching Fury: Voices of the Storm, 1820–1861* (New York: HarperCollins, 1997), 38.

28 *Evening Star*, June 21, 1869, facsimile at Historical Society of Washington, D.C.

29 Allen C. Clark, "The Trollopes," *Records of the Columbia Historical Society of Washington, D.C.* 37, 38 (1937): 79–100.

30 The United States maintained an army of sixteen thousand soldiers, most of them scattered over the Pacific Coast, Utah, and the Southwest.

31 Margaret Leech, *Reveille in Washington, 1860–1865* (New York: Harper & Bros., 1941), 3.

32 Ibid., 128.

33 Ibid., 174; and Katharine Prescott Wormeley, *The Other Side of the War: With the Army of the Potomac* (Boston: Ticknor and Co., 1889).

34 Union general Benjamin Butler first used this expression.

35 Kathryn Allamong Jacob, *Capital Elites: High Society in Washington, D.C., After the Civil War* (Washington, D.C.: Smithsonian Institution Press, 1995), 50.

36 David Herbert Donald, *Lincoln* (New York: Simon and Schuster, 1995), 431.

37 Richard Dobbins, American Civil War Research Database, Historical Data Systems, Inc., www.civilwardata.com.

38 Edward Chase Kirkland, *Charles Francis Adams, Jr., 1835–1915: The Patrician at Bay* (Cambridge, MA: Harvard University Press, 1965), 29, 30.

39 Charles Francis Adams, *Charles Francis Adams: An Autobiography* (Boston: Houghton Mifflin, 1916), 165, 166.

40 Ira Berlin, ed., *The Black Military Experience* (New York: Cambridge University Press, 1982).

41 William McFeely, *Frederick Douglass* (New York: W. W. Norton, 1991), 257.

42 Emory Smith, "Lost and Found, Not Dead but Living: Howard's First Graduate, James T. Wormley, '70Ph.,'" *The Howard Alumnus* (January 1927): 82, 83.

43 M. F. Perkins, "Francis Grimke," *Journal of Negro History* 21, no. 1 (January 1936): 57.

44 Charles Francis Adams, the wartime minister to London, had tried unsuccessfully to persuade the British government to make retribution with a monetary settlement. After Adams was recalled in 1868, Andrew Johnson's next minister, Reverdy Johnson, worked out a moderate compromise with Lord Clarendon, the British foreign secretary. But Reverdy Johnson was out of favor with the Republicans in the Senate, so shortly after Grant's inauguration, on August 13, 1869, the Johnson-Clarendon Convention was rejected by the Senate.

45 "The Marriage of Paul Gerard and the Pretty Octoroon," *Evening Star*, December 8, 1869.

46 Riggs Bank Archives, total loans for 1870: $10,890.97; endorsers besides Riggs and Robeson were: D. C. Forney, J. R. Sawyer, J. B. Ward, Beckwith Huntley, C. Gautier. Total loans for 1871: $3,845.75; endorsers: Riggs, Gautier, Dickson King, Shomaker Hertzog, E. E. Randall, Lewis C. Kengla. Archivist Mary Beth Corrigan made my visit to the archives possible and kindly provided ledgers that had Wormley's records.

47 Quoted in Thomas R. Johnson, "The City on the Hill: Race Relations in Washington, D.C.," (PhD diss., University of Maryland, 1975), ii.

48 Minutes, General Term 1, Supreme Court of the District of Columbia, Selection of Jurors, October 9, 1871, p. 569, National Records Center, Suitland, MD, Wormley Papers, 569, CD-ROM.

49 The secretary of the interior was reluctant to appoint William Wormley because of his "want of education." Thirty-three years old in 1870, Wormley had already been superintendent of the Sabbath School Union for three years. Owing to strong letters of support, Wormley got the appointment.

50 Edward Ingle, *The Negro in the District of Columbia* (Baltimore: Johns Hopkins Press, 1893), 91.

51 Dr. Gamaliel Bailey came to Washington, D.C., in 1847 to assume leadership of the *National Era*, a new four-page paper intended to promote the anti-slavery movement. It was published until March 1860.

52 Copy of letter belonging to Donet Graves, James T. Wormley's great-grandson, Massachusetts Historical Society.

Chapter 2. Grant's Second Administration and Needed Reform

1 Grant: 3,597,070; Greeley: 2,834,079 (44 percent).

2 James M. McPherson, "Grant or Greeley? The Abolitionist Dilemma in the Election of 1872," *American Historical Review* 71 (October 1965): 51.

3 Willard H. Smith, *Schuyler Colfax: The Changing Fortunes of a Political Idol* (Indianapolis: Indiana Historical Bureau, 1952).

4 Why the marriage ended so quickly no one knows. There were several rumors at the time, predominantly that Sumner was impotent and that Alice was linked romantically with Baron Friedrich von Holstein. Sumner's potency was pure speculation; the Alice Mason Hooper link to Baron Holstein is false.

5 David Herbert Donald, *Charles Sumner* (New York: Da Capo Press, 1996), 586; Edward L. Pierce in *Memoir and Letters of Charles Sumner* (Boston: Roberts Brothers, 1894), iv, 596–99, gives a slightly different account of Sumner's last hours. "The servants heard a noise as from a fall and one of them going to the senator's chamber found him . . . apparently suffering severe pain. A doctor was sent for; he administered morphine. His friends, Wormley and H.L. Pierce, who lived nearby, were notified of his condition, and came at once to the house." In the morning, before sunrise, other doctors and friends and colleagues were sent for. Wormley, "serving as friendly nurse," remained until the end, which came "thirteen minutes before three" p.m.

6 Donald, *Charles Sumner*, 9.

7 *Railroad Company v. Brown*, 87 U.S. 445 (1873).

8 Donald, *Charles Sumner*, 10.

9 Ibid., 547–48.

10 Timothy Rives, "Grant, Babcock, and the Whiskey Ring," *Prologue: Quarterly of the National Archives and Records Administration* 32, no. 3 (Fall 2000), http://www.nara.gov.

11 Ibid., 5.

12 Ibid., 6.

13 Dee Alexander Brown, "The William Belknap Scandal," *National Historical Society* 4 (1969): 34, 35.

14 Robert Wild, "The Belknap Impeachment Trial," *Wisconsin Magazine of History* 10 (December 1926): 213.

15 Ibid., 216.

16 44th Congress, 1st session, House Reports, no. 799, 76–86.

17 Wild, "The Belknap Impeachment Trial," 212.

18 Ibid., 215.

19 William S. McFeely, *Grant: A Biography* (New York: W. W. Norton, 1981), 406.

20 Jacob, *Capital Elites*, 90.

21 Jonathan Kandell, "Boss," *Smithsonian* (February 2002): 87.

22 Alexander Flick, *Samuel Jones Tilden: A Study in Political Sagacity* (New York: Dodd, Mead, and Co., 1939), 199.

23 Edwin Burrows and Mike Wallace, *Gotham: A History of New York City to 1898* (New York: Oxford University Press, 1999), 931.

24 Alexander Callow Jr., *The Tweed Ring* (New York: Oxford University Press, 1966), 203.

25 Flick, *Samuel Jones Tilden*, 221.

26 Ibid., 219.

27 Ibid., 225.

Chapter 3. In the Blink of an Eye

1 Notes from *The Measure of a Man: James Wormley, a Nineteenth-Century African-American Entrepreneur*, an exhibit presented by the Historical Society of Washington, D.C., February 19–May 1, 1993.

2 James H. Whyte, *The Uncivil War: Washington During Reconstruction* (New York: Twayne, 1958), 113.

3 Ibid., 175.

4 Constance McLaughlin Green, *The Secret City: A History of Race Relations in the Nation's Capital* (Princeton, NJ: Princeton University Press, 1967), 105.

5 Whyte, *The Uncivil War*, 212.

6 Green, *Secret City*, 113.

7 According to Boyd's Directory of Washington and Georgetown for 1867, the addresses of the properties James Wormley owned on I Street were: 310, 314, 318, 320 I Street North, between Fifteenth and Sixteenth Streets West. This numbering system was replaced by the current system, which would place the sites in the 1500 block of I Street, NW.

8 For facts about Tenleytown and the Wormley farm, I am indebted to Judith Beck Helm, *Tenleytown, D.C.: Country Village Into City Neighborhood* (Washington, D.C.: Tennally Press, 1981).

9 In 1929, when Van Ness Street had replaced much of Pierce Mill Road, Reno Road was cut through only north of the Bureau of Standards, going toward Chevy Chase. Van Ness Street maintained the curve of the old road east of Reno Road in order to avoid cutting down the large, old beech and oak trees so precious to the Wormleys. Helm, *Tenleytown, D.C.*, 386.

10 Alex to Walton E. Shipley on Pope Ballard & Loos stationery, June 26, 1974. Courtesy of Freida Wormley.

11 Francis Grimké to G. Smith Wormley, August 23, 1934, *Journal of Negro History* 21, 1 (January 1936): 57.

12 Francis Grimké to Dr. C. G. Woodson, August 23, 1934, *Journal of Negro History* 21, 1 (January 1936): 58–59.

13 *Charles Sumner: His Complete Works* (New York: Negro Universities Press, 1969), 181. Originally published in 1900 by Lee and Shepard.

14 *Journal of Negro History* 21 (January 1936): 58.

15 J. A. Truesdall, Communications, *Washington Post*, July 13, 187? (year is illegible). Item found in Wormley scrapbooks, courtesy of Freida Wormley.

16 Ibid.

17 Keith Melder, *City of Magnificent Intentions: A History of Washington, District of Columbia* (Washington, D.C.: Intac, 1983), 58.

18 R. Frank Jones, MD, *Trials of a Pioneer*, paper presented before the American Urological Association, May 20, 1978.

19 Henry Robinson, "Some Aspects of the Free Negro Population of Washington, D.C., 1800–1862," *Maryland Historical Magazine* (Spring 1969): 58.

20 Interview with Miriam Wormley Lewis, daughter of W. H. A. Wormley and granddaughter of James Wormley, November 29, 1976. Interview conducted by Stanton Wormley Sr., Wormley Papers, CD-ROM.

21 Morris J. MacGregor, *The Emergence of a Black Catholic Community: St. Augustine's in Washington* (Washington, D.C.: Catholic University of America Press, 1999).

22 Robinson, "Some Aspects of the Free Negro Population of Washington, D.C.," 54.

23 *New National Era*, October 9, 1873, quoted in Green, *Secret City*, 372, 373.

24 Civil Rights Act of 1866 passed by the 39th Congress.

25 Foner, *A Short History of Reconstruction*, 224.

26 Ibid.

27 Loren Miller, *The Petitioners: The Story of the Supreme Court of the United States and the Negro* (New York: Pantheon, 1966), 108.

28   Peter Irons, *A People's History of the Supreme Court* (New York: Viking, 1999), 203.

29   John R. Howard, *The Shifting Wind: The Supreme Court and Civil Rights from Reconstruction to Brown* (Albany: State University Press of New York, 1999), 99.

30   Robert M. Goldman, *Reconstruction and Black Suffrage: Losing the Vote in Reese and Cruikshank* (Lawrence: University Press of Kansas, 2001), 91, 95.

31   Howard, *Shifting Wind*, 109.

32   William Gillette, *Retreat from Reconstruction, 1869–1879* (Baton Rouge: Louisiana State University Press, 1979), 310.

Chapter 4. Election

1   A favorite son is a person favored for nomination as a presidential candidate by his own state delegates at a national political convention for at least the first ballot.

2   "Vice Presidents of the United States, William A. Wheeler," http://www.senate.gov /artandhistory/history/resources/pdf/william_wheeler.pdf.

3   Lloyd Robinson, *The Stolen Election: Hayes versus Tilden 1876* (Garden City, NY: Doubleday, 1968), 64.

4   Ibid., 58, 59.

5   As a former governor, Noyes gave the welcoming speech to the convention, held in Cincinnati. Quoted in Roy Morris Jr., *Fraud of the Century* (New York: Simon and Schuster, 2003), 72.

6   Quoted in Sister Mary Karl George, R.S.M., *Zachariah Chandler: A Political Biography* (East Lansing: Michigan State University Press, 1969), 250.

7   Ibid., 251.

8   Keith Ian Polakoff, *The Politics of Inertia: The Election of 1876 and the End of Reconstruction* (Baton Rouge: Louisiana State University Press, 1973), 138.

9   Ibid.

10   Allan Nevins, *Abram S. Hewitt* (New York: Octagon Books, 1967), 317.

11   Ibid., 28.

12   According to Roy Morris Jr. in *Fraud of the Century: Rutherford B. Hayes and the Stolen Election of 1876* (New York: Simon and Schuster, 2003), 11, "Ever since the day in 1868 when Massachusetts congressman Benjamin F. Butler had flourished on the floor of Congress the torn and blood-stained shirt of a federal tax collector whipped by the Ku Klux Klan in Mississippi, the bloody shirt had become the Republican party's most effective propaganda weapon."

13   Dee Alexander Brown, *The Year of the Century: 1876* (New York: Scribner, 1966), 233.

14 Rutherford B. Hayes to James A. Garfield, August 5, 1876, Polakoff, *Politics of Inertia*, 115.

15 Nevins, *Abram S. Hewitt*, 313.

16 Bill Severn, *Samuel J. Tilden and the Stolen Election* (New York: Ives Washburn, 1968), 170.

17 Jerome Sternstein, "The Sickles Memorandum: Another Look at the Hayes-Tilden Election Night Conspiracy," *Journal of Southern History* 32 (August 1966): 342–57.

18 Polakoff, *Politics of Inertia*, 200.

19 Nevins, *Abram S. Hewitt*, 322.

20 Henry Watterson, *Marse Henry: An Autobiography*, http://metalab.unc.edu/docsouth /watterson, 119 (accessed July 19, 2000) (292 print version).

21 William Rehnquist, *Centennial Crisis: The Disputed Election of 1876* (New York: Alfred Knopf, 2004), 106.

22 John R. Howard, *Shifting Wind*, 110; and *New York Times*, November 15, 23, 27, and 29, 1876.

23 Ibid.

24 William Ivy Hair, *Bourbonism and Agrarian Protest: Louisiana Politics, 1877–1900* (Baton Rouge: Louisiana State University Press, 1969), 7.

25 Ari Hoogenboom, *Rutherford B. Hayes: Warrior and President* (Lawrence: University Press of Kansas, 1995), 5 (electronic edition). See esp. chapter 17.

26 Watterson, *Marse Henry*, 121 (electronic edition); 292 (print edition).

27 Roy Morris Jr. says twenty-five Republicans and twenty Democrats.

28 Nevins, *Abram S. Hewitt*, 330.

29 Watterson, *Marse Henry*, 293 (print edition).

30 Joe Gray Taylor, *Louisiana Reconstructed, 1863–1877* (Baton Rouge: Louisiana State University Press, 1974), 491.

31 Watterson, *Marse Henry*, 121, 122 (electronic edition); 298, 299 (print edition).

32 Abram S. Hewitt Papers, 1803–1903, Cooper Archives, Cooper Union Library, v. 41.

33 Cipher telegrams cited in Hearings of Clarkson Potter Committee, House of Representatives, 1878.

34 Ibid.

35 Hoogenboom, *Rutherford B. Hayes*, 5 (electronic edition).

36 Polakoff, *Politics of Inertia*, 216; and Jerrell H. Shofner, *Nor Is It Over Yet: Florida in the Era of Reconstruction* (Gainesville: University of Florida, 1974), 318.

37   W. H. Roberts, quoted in Roy Morris Jr., *Fraud of the Century*, 207

38   Nevins, *Abram S. Hewitt*, 335.

39   Hewitt Papers, acc. 3104.

Chapter 5. We, the Other People

1   Robert C. Post, ed., *1876: A Centennial Exhibition* (Washington, D.C.: Smithsonian Press, 1976), 11.

2   John Maass, *The Glorious Enterprise: The Centennial Exhibition of 1876 and H.J. Swarzmann, Architect-in-Chief* (Watkins Glen, NY: American Life Foundation, 1973), 28.

3   Thomas Schlereth, in "The Philadelphia Centennial as Teaching Model," *Hayes Historical Journal* 1, no. 3 (1977): 203, says that fifty-six nations eventually accepted.

4   Dee Brown, *The Year of the Century: 1876* (New York: Charles Scribner's Sons, 1966), 121.

5   Maass, *Glorious Enterprise*, 118.

6   Dee Brown, in *Year of the Century*, 121, says King Kalakava of the Sandwich Islands also had been in the United States.

7   Thomas Cochran to Elizabeth Duane Gillespie, June 9, 1875, in Maass, *The Glorious Enterprise*, 121.

8   *New York Times*, May 8, 1875, quoted in John Hicks, "The United States Centennial Exhibition of 1876" (PhD diss., University of Georgia, 1972), 9.

9   Ibid., 92, 93.

10   *New York Tribune*, July 6, 1876.

11   Robert A. Trennert Jr., "A Grand Failure: The Centennial Indian Exhibition of 1876," *Prologue* 6, no. 2 (Summer 1974): 129.

12   William Dean Howells, "A Sennight of the Centennial," *Atlantic Monthly* 38 (1876): 103, quoted in H. Craig Miner, "The United States Government Building at the Centennial Exhibition, 1874–77," *Prologue* 4 (Winter 1972): 211.

13   Ibid.

14   Robert Rydell, *All the World's a Fair: Visions of Empire at American International Expositions, 1876–1916* (Chicago: University of Chicago Press, 1984), 27.

15   Ibid.

16   Trennert, "A Grand Failure," 125.

17   Letter appeared March 16, 1872; quoted in Mitch Kachun, "Before the Eyes of All Nations: African-American Identity and Historical Memory at the Centennial Exposition of 1876," *Pennsylvania History* 65, no. 3 (Summer 1998): 309.

18   Ibid., 311.

19   Ibid., 309.

20   Philip Foner, "Black Participation in the Centennial of 1876," *Negro History Bulletin* 36 (February 1976): 534.

21   From "A Sennight at the Centennial," quoted in Ducarmel Augustin, "African Americans During the 1876 Centennial Exposition," *The Centennial Exhibition of 1876: A Material Culture Study by Villanova University Students* (Villanova, PA: Villanova University, 1998), www3.villanova.edu/centennial/daugus01.html.

22   Mitch Kachun, "The Faith That the Dark Past Has Taught Us: African-American Commemorations in the North and West and The Construction of a Usable Past" (PhD diss., Cornell, 1997), 357.

23   Rutherford B. Hayes, "The Hayes-Tilden Campaign–June," ed. Charles Richard Williams, *The Diary and Letters of Rutherford B. Hayes* (Columbus: Ohio State Archeological and Historical Society, 1922), 38. Electronic edition found at www.ohiohistory.org/onlinedoc/hayes/chapterxxxiii.html.

24   Rydell, *All the World's a Fair*, 29.

25   Eric Foner, *Reconstruction: America's Unfinished Revolution, 1863–1877* (New York: Harper and Row, 1988), 162.

26   Bruno Giberti, *Designing the Centennial: A History of the 1876 International Exhibition in Philadelphia* (Lexington: University Press of Kentucky, 2002), 96.

27   Photocopy of letter and ticket courtesy of Donet Graves, great-great-grandson of James Wormley.

28   Melvil Dewey, originator of the Dewey Decimal Classification used in libraries to this day, published his system in a pamphlet in 1876. He copied his system from Blake's centennial classification, and for his imaginative application he deserves credit, but for his failure to acknowledge his debt to Blake, he merits censure.

29   Rydell, *All the World's a Fair*, 22.

30   Ibid., 29.

Chapter 6. Resolution of Election

Most of the facts in this chapter come from reading records at the National Archives of the House Select Committees of the 44th and 45th Congresses, including the minutes of May 22, 1878, to March 3, 1879, of the Select Committee on Alleged Frauds in the Late Presidential Election of 1876. Boxes most helpful in relation to the election and the Electoral Commission include:

HR 44A-F39.2 (Privileges and Duties in the House in the counting of electoral votes)
HR 44A-H20.33 to HR 44A-H21.2

HR 44A-H21.2
HR 44A-H21.3
HR 44A-31
HR 45A-F37.1, folders 1-25

1   Rutherford B. Hayes in diary, January 1, 1877, T. Harry Williams, ed., *Hayes: The Diary of a President, 1875–1881* (New York: David McKay Company, 1964), 65, 66.

2   Allan Nevins, *Hamilton Fish: The Inner History of the Grant Administration* (New York: Frederick Ungar Publishing, 1937, 1956), 2:851.

3   Ibid.

4   Ibid., 85.

5   Milton Harlow Northrup, "A Grave Crisis in American History: The Inner History of the Origins and Formation of the Electoral Commission of 1877," *Century Magazine* 62 (October 1901): 932.

6   Ibid., 929.

7   Alan Dowty, "David Davis and the Hayes-Tilden Contest, 1876–77" (master's thesis, University of Chicago, 1960), 55, 56.

8   Keith Ian Polakoff, *Politics of Inertia*, 251–56; C. Vann Woodward in *Reunion and Reaction: The Compromise of 1877 and the End of Reconstruction* (Boston: Little, Brown, 1951), accurately described a Republican effort to break Democratic unity in the South. Although his account, that the WAP effort led directly to the Wormley Compromise or Compromise of 1877, had been accepted for almost a half a century, two historians recently have shown that Woodward's evidence was faulty.

9   Foner, *A Short History of Reconstruction*, 243.

10   Sidney Pomerantz, "Election of 1876," ed. Arthur Schlesinger Jr. and Fred Israel, *History of American Presidential Elections, 1789–1968* (New York: Chelsea House, 1971), 2:1416.

11   Michael Les Benedict, "Southern Democrats in the Crisis of 1876–1877: A Reconsideration of *Reunion and Reaction*," *Journal of Southern History* (November 1980): 509.

12   Woodward in *Reunion and Reaction* made the point that a definite bargain between Northern Republicans and "Whiggish" Southern Democrats was struck primarily over national help in building the Texas and Pacific Railroad. Benedict in an essay, "Southern Democrats in the Crisis of 1876–1877," shows that actual voting patterns of Southern Democrats in the electoral count controversy and of Southern opinion during the crisis indicates Woodward described accurately a Republican effort to break down Democratic unity in the South, but the evidence Woodward used rested on the correspondence of William Henry Smith, Henry Van Ness Boynton, and Andrew Kellar. However, these men overestimated or exaggerated the strength of the Scott lobby. The outright bargain Woodward described did not take place, Benedict rightly concludes.

13   The House of Representatives chose Henry Payne of Ohio, Eppa Hunton of Virginia, and Josiah Abbot of Massachusetts, all Democrats, and George Hoar of Massachusetts and James Garfield of Ohio, Republicans, as the House's commissioners. The Senate chose George Edmunds of Vermont, Frederick Frelinghuysen of New Jersey, and Oliver Morton of Indiana, all Republicans, and Allen Thurman of Ohio and Thomas Bayard of Delaware, Democrats, as the Senate's commissioners. The four associate justices of the Supreme Court were Nathan Clifford and Stephen Field, Democrats; and William Strong and Samuel Miller, Republicans. They offered the fifth place to David Davis, Independent, who declined, and then to Joseph Bradley, Republican.

14   Brainerd Dyer, *The Public Career of William M. Evarts* (New York: Da Capo Press, 1969), 175.

15   Pomerantz, "Election of 1876," 1418.

16   T. Harry Williams, *Hayes*, 73.

17   H. J. Eckenrode, *Rutherford Hayes: Statesman of Reunion* (New York: Dodd, Mead and Co., 1930), 215.

18   Burke's testimony, Potter Committee's Presidential Election Investigation, vol. 1, 962.

19   Letter of William E. Chandler, http://memory.loc.gov/cgi-bin/query/D?mrray:3:/temp /___ ammenZEQgm.

20   Burke to Nicholls, February 26, 1877, House Miscellaneous Documents, 45th Cong., 3 sess. Doc. No. 31, Vol. 3, 598.

21   Dyer, *Public Career*, 179.

22   *New York Tribune*, February 15, 1978, 1; Ari Hoogenboom, *Rutherford B. Hayes: Warrior and President* (Lawrence: University Press of Kansas, 1995), 17.

23   In some accounts of the meeting at Wormley's, given years or decades after the fact, say that R. C. Gibson of Louisiana was also present.

24   Garfield's diary, February 26, 1877, quoted in Keith Ian Polakoff, *Politics of Inertia*, 311.

25   Ibid.

26   Robert Cinnamond Tucker, "The Life and Public Service of E. John Ellis," *Louisiana Historical Quarterly* 29 (July 1946): 735.

27   Ibid., 736.

28   Pomerantz, "Election of 1876," 1471.

29   Ibid.

30   Polakoff, *Politics of Inertia*, 310, 311.

31   Nevins, *Abram S. Hewitt, With Some Account of Peter Cooper* (New York: Octagon Books, 1967), 383; and in "A Narrative of Facts in Connection with the Presidential Campaign of 1876 and Action of the Electoral Commission Constituted by Congress in 1877," Abram Hewitt Papers, New York Historical Society, acc. 3104; also printed in *Selected Writing of Abram S. Hewitt*, ed. Allan Nevins (New York: Columbia University Press, 1937).

32   Woodward, *Reunion and Reaction*, 201.

33   Nevins, *Hewitt, With Some Account*, 385.

34   Tucker, "The Life and Public Service of E. John Ellis," 732.

35   Vincent de Santis, "Rutherford B. Hayes and the Removal of Troops and the End of Reconstruction," eds. J. Morgan Kousser and James McPherson, *Region, Race, and Reconstruction: Essays in Honor of C. Vann Woodward* (New York: Oxford University Press, 1982), 443.

36   Nevins, *Hamilton Fish*, 858.

37   Hair, *Bourbonism and Agrarian Protest*.

38   All four members of the Louisiana Returning Board were indicted; only T. C. Anderson of Opelousas was convicted and later pardoned. The other three never went on trial.

39   Santis, "Rutherford B. Hayes and the Removal of Troops and the End of Reconstruction," 417.

40   Henry Watterson, quoted in de Santis, "Rutherford B. Hayes and the Removal of Troops and the End of Reconstruction," 428.

41   Ibid.

42   These views have been expertly argued by Foner in *A Short History of Reconstruction* and by Gillette in *Retreat from Reconstruction*.

43   Hayes to Bryan, July 8, 1876, quoted in de Santis, "Rutherford B. Hayes and the Removal of Troops and the End of Reconstruction," 441.

Chapter 7. States' Rights Ride Supreme

1   Vincent De Santis, "President Hayes's Southern Policy," *Journal of Southern History* 21, no. 4 (November 1955): 480.

2   Ernest Samuels, *Henry Adams* (Cambridge, MA: Belknap Press of Harvard University Press, 1989), 128.

3   Alan Trachtenberg, *The Incorporation of America: Culture and Society in the Gilded Age* (New York: Hill and Wang, 1982), 41.

4   Gillette, *Retreat from Reconstruction*, 348.

5   Rayford Logan, *The Betrayal of the Negro: From Rutherford B. Hayes to Woodrow Wilson* (London: Collier Books, 1954), 23–47.

6   Charles Wynes, "James Wormley of the Wormley Hotel Agreement," *Centennial Review* (Winter 1875): 399.

7   Arline Boucher Tehan, *Henry Adams in Love* (New York: Universe Books, 1983).

8   Henry Adams to James Wormley, June 12, 1878, Massachusetts Historical Society Collection #MSS-130, copies of originals belonging to Donet Graves.

9   Kenneth D. Ackerman, *Dark Horse: The Surprise Election and Political Murder of President James A. Garfield* (New York: Carroll and Graf, 2003).

10 Letitia Brown and Elsie Lewis, *Washington in the New Era, 1870–1970* (Washington D.C.: Smithsonian, 1972), 7.

11 Sidney Pomerantz, "Election of 1876," ed. Arthur Schlesinger Jr. and Fred Israel, *History of American Presidential Elections, 1789–1968* (New York: Chelsea House, 1971), 2:1434.

12 Foner, *Reconstruction*, 587.

13 David L. Lewis, *District of Columbia: A Bicentennial History* (New York: W. W. Norton, 1976), 71.

14 Michael Ross, *Justice of Shattered Dreams: Samuel Freeman Miller and the Supreme Court During the Civil War Era* (Baton Rouge: Louisiana State University Press, 2003), 248.

15 "A Noted Hotel Keeper Dead," *New York Daily Tribune*, October 19, 1884; "Arrival of the Remains in This City—Arangements for the Funeral," *Washington Post*, October 20, 1884.

16 Cleveland *Plain Dealer*, October 25, 1884.

17 Notes that accompanied *The Measure of a Man* exhibit.

18 Georgetown University bought the old and decrepit Wormley School in 1997 and then put it up for sale in March 2005. The building had been vacant since 1994. Today, it has been converted into condos.

19 *Washington Post* ad in scrapbooks of Stanton L. Wormley, courtesy of Freida H. Wormley, Washington, D.C.

20 Betty Randall, "Wormley's Hotel: A Reflection of the Reconstruction Period." Article in Stanton Wormley's papers, courtesy Freida Wormley, Washington, D.C.

21 The Wormley School closed in 1952, so the school board gave the portrait to Charles Sumner Wormley. Today it hangs in the Historic Society of Washington, D.C.

22 Helm, *Tenleytown*, 203.

23   In 1897 Wormley's was renamed the Colonial. In 1906 the structure was torn down to make way for the Union Trust building, which still occupies the site.

24   James McPherson, *Ordeal by Fire: The Civil War and Reconstruction* (New York: Alfred Knopf, 1982), 618. The grandfather clause was nullified by the Supreme Court in 1915.

25   Like Uncle Tom of the minstrel shows that followed in the wake of Harriet Beecher Stowe's novel, *Uncle Tom's Cabin*, the term "Jim Crow" came from a white man in blackface. A white entertainer named Thomas Dartmouth Rice wrote a song-and-dance tune about a Negro named Jim Crow that became an international hit in the 1830s. Before long Jim Crow became a synonym for Negro.

26   Brown and Lewis, *Washington in the New Era*, 31, 32.

27   David W. Blight, *Race and Reunion: The Civil War in American Memory* (Cambridge, MA: Belknap Press of Harvard University Press, 2001), 358.

28   In January of 1950, Mary Church Terrell, a human rights activist in her late eighties; Reverend W. H. Jernigan, pastor of the Mt. Carmel Church; Geneva Brown, treasurer of the United Cafeteria and Restaurant Workers Union; David Scull, a member of the Society of Friends; Reverend Arthur Fletcher Elmes, pastor of the People's Congregational Church; and Essie Thompson, United Cafeteria and Restaurant Workers Union, went to Thompson's Restaurant at 725 Fourteenth Street, NW, to eat. They were refused service. No surprise. In fact, they counted on it. They were all members of the Coordinating Committee for the Enforcement of the D.C. Anti-Discrimination Laws. CCEAD was organized in 1949, to bring to the attention of the public and city officials the 1872 and 1873 laws that made discrimination in public places in Washington, D.C., illegal. The "lost laws," as they were known, had been removed after Reconstruction ended. They were rediscovered in the 1940s, and the CCEAD sought to have these laws reinstated. Through their efforts, on June 8, 1953, the Supreme Court ruled that the 1872 and 1873 laws were still valid, declaring that segregation in public places was illegal.

29   John T. Noonan Jr., *Narrowing the Nation's Power: The Supreme Court Sides with the States* (Berkeley: University of California Press, 2002), 129 ff.

Epilogue

1   Nicholas Kristof, "America's 'Primal Scream,'" *New York Times*, October 16, 2011.

2   Jeffrey Rosen, "The Unregulated Offensive," *New York Times Magazine* (April 17, 2005): 45.

3   Had the recount continued, as later studied by the *New York Times* and the *Miami Herald*, Gore would have won Florida by 209 votes. Exceptions to this assessment were Martin Merzer, "Review of Ballots Finds Bush's Win Would Have Endured Manual Recounts," *Miami Herald*, April 4, 2001; and Dan Keating and Dan Balz, "Florida

Recounts Would Have Favored Bush, But Study Finds Gore Might Have Won Statewide Talley of All Uncounted Ballots," *Washington Post*, November 12, 2001. For an overall account of the voting and recounting, see the report issued by the U.S. Commission on Civil Rights, *Voting Irregularities in Florida During the 2000 Presidential Election*, www.usccr.gov/pubs/vote2000/report/main.htm.

4   Noonan, *Narrowing the Nation's Power*, 129 ff.

5   Peter Irons, *A People's History of the Supreme Court* (New York: Viking, 2002), 95.

6   Ibid.

7   Elaine Cassel, "Expanding the States' Rights at the Cost of Federal Law Guarantees: A Review of Judge John T. Noonan's *Narrowing the Nation's Power: The Supreme Court Sides with the States*," *Law Book Reviews*, November 22, 2002.

8   http://leahy.senate.gov/press/20210/100102.html and http://judiciary.senate.gov/.

9   Quoted in Noonan, *Narrowing the Nation's Power*.

10   Quoted in Mark S. Mulholland, "Bi-Partisan Support for Restoration of Federal Intellectual Property Infringement Remedies," www.rmfpc.com.

11   Hearing on *Narrowing the Nation's Power: The Supreme Court Sides with the States* Before Senate Committee on the Judiciary, 107th Cong.(2002) (statement of Senator Leahy).

12   "Sovereign Immunity vs. Justice," *World View Commentary* no. 38, June 30, 1999, Center for International Human Rights.

13   Simon Lazarus, "The Court Runs Amok," *Blueprint, Ideas for a New Century*, December 2, 2002, http://www.dlc.org/ndol_ci.cfm?kaid=127&subid=177&contentid =251056.

14   Aruna Viswanatha, "Supreme Court Limits 'Honest Services' Law," *Main Justice, Politics, Policy and the Law* (June 24, 2010), http://www.mainjustice.com/2010/06/24 /supreme-court-limits-honest-services-law/.

15   Eric Foner, *Who Owns History? Rethinking the Past in a Changing World* (New York: Hill and Wang, 2002), 183.

INDEX

ABOUT THE AUTHOR

Carol Gelderman retired as Distinguished Professor of English at the University of New Orleans, where she taught nonfiction writing and modern drama. She is the author of nine previous books, including the biographies *Henry Ford: The Wayward Capitalist* (Dial Press, St. Martin's Press); *Mary McCarthy: A Life* (St. Martin's Press, Sidwick & Jackson, London); and *Louis Auchincloss: A Writer's Life* (Crown, University of South Carolina Press). The Ford biography was scripted into a four-part television series, financed by the MacArthur Foundation and by the National Endowment for the Humanities Planning and Production grants. *Mary McCarthy*, a *New York Times* Outstanding Book of the Year, was also cited by the booksellers of England as "the best literary biography of Great Britain in 1989." A 1997 book, *All the Presidents' Words: The Bully Pulpit and the Creation of the Virtual Presidency*, details the effects that presidential speechwriters and "spin doctoring" have had on public policymaking. This book was also a *New York Times* Outstanding Book of the Year.

Gelderman has also written dozens of articles on topics as varied as theater, biography, government, and mutual funds for publications such as *Presidential Studies*, the *Antioch Review*, the *Wilson Quarterly*, the *Chronicle of Higher Education*, *American Theatre*, *Encyclopedia Britannica*, *McGraw-Hill Encyclopedia of World Drama*, and *Scribner's Encyclopedia of American Legislative Systems*, and in newspapers such as the *Times-Picayune*.

She has also served as an on-air commentator in documentaries on several topics, including presidential speechwriting for a PBS piece; on the modern theater for Maryland Public TV's twenty-six-part series *Literary Visions*; on NHK Education Corporation's series on American writers for Tokyo TV; and a piece on Henry Ford and anti-Semitism for Guggenheim Productions' PBS series *Shadow of Hate*, sponsored by the Southern Poverty Law Center.

Finally, Gelderman has participated as panelist and/or keynoter at venues like the Smithsonian, Heritage Foundation, Williams College, Kennedy School of Government at Harvard, the New Orleans Writers' Conference, and the Tennessee Williams Literary Festival.